FANATICAL

Tom Hoefner

I0139578

BROADWAY PLAY PUBLISHING INC
New York
www.broadwayplaypublishing.com
info@broadwayplaypublishing.com

FANATICAL
© Copyright 2023 Tom Hoefner

Cover art by Kevin Gillespie

First edition: January 2023
I S B N: 978-0-88145-956-2

Book design: Marie Donovan
Page make-up: Adobe InDesign
Typeface: Palatino

CHARACTERS & SETTING

GINA
STANLEY
BRUCE GLOVER
RICK HERNANDEZ
NATALIE CRANE
POLICE COMMISSIONER
JEB DUTT
SHERMAN SCHNEIDER
YANO
KYLA KERNEY
PATTY AMADA
POLICEMAN

a basement

ACT ONE

Prologue

(As the house fades to black, a music cue blares to life: it is the title anthem from Space Corps, the legendary sci-fi/ fantasy film franchise. As the "Space Corps March" plays, a NARRATOR *speaks in a deep voice.)*

(Author's Note: If possible, this piece of narration should be projected on a screen as a scrolling block of text.)

NARRATOR *(VO)* It is a time of unrest.

Bruce Glover, the creator and director of the *Space Corps* series of films, has fallen out of favor with his most diehard fans.

With production about to begin on *Space Corps Chapter 6* and the future of a billion dollar franchise at stake, Bruce's company, GloverFilm, has dispatched Bruce to speak at the annual Pasadena Comic Book Convention, hoping to alleviate the very serious and important concerns shared by *Space Corps* devotees across the globe.

Unknown to Bruce, a pair of *Space Corps* superfans, self-appointed guardians of narrative, tone, and plot devices, will also attend the convention, and they have a plan...

(The fanfare fades out.)

Scene 1

(Lights up)

(A basement. Furnished, but clearly a basement. USC is a staircase that climbs up the wall from SL and leads to a first floor doorway. Under the staircase is another door, leading to an offstage boiler room. SR, a doorway leads to a small bathroom.)

(The basement is carpeted. It has a couch and an end table and a couple of big shelving units and fancy display cases. The entire room: throw rug, couch pillows, posters, model spaceships, books, scale prop replicas...everything is decorated with memorabilia and officially licensed merchandise from the mega blockbuster fantasy film franchise Space Corps!)

(There is also a mini-fridge and an old radiator against the SR wall.)

(The door at the top of the stairs kicks open, and an odd procession marches in and down the steps. Two head-to-toe armored Corps Fighters [the foot soldiers of Space Corps' evil Solar Monarchy] come before and behind a captured Kookoochik [a sentient space bear], the Kookoochik's arms secured in binders. Fighter #1, standing in front, is leading the Kookoochik by a chain secured around its neck. Fighter #2 brings up the rear, and is holding a sci-fi blaster rifle lazily in one hand.)

(The Corps Fighters march the Kookoochik, who is wobbly as he goes, down the steps and towards the door under the stairs. Fighter #1 opens the door as Fighter #2 pushes the Kookoochik in. Fighter #1 shuts the door.)

(The Corps Fighters look at each other. Fighter #1 [GINA] speaks.)

GINA: You're holding it wrong.

STANLEY: What?

(GINA *points at the blaster rifle that* STANLEY *[Fighter #2]*
is holding with one hand, like a pistol.)

GINA: The TS-620. You're holding it wrong. You're
holding it like a pistol. It's a rifle.

(STANLEY *shifts his grip on his rifle to a two-handed grip.*)

STANLEY: Doh. Right.

GINA: You were doing that on the convention floor,
too. I was terrified someone would notice.

STANLEY: Of course, sorry. I'm an idiot. (*He takes off his*
helmet.) Hurry up, let's go.

(*They quickly begin stripping off their armor, taking off*
their helmets first. Underneath the helmets are GINA *and*
STANLEY, *both in their 30s. They are giddy. Underneath*
their armor they are in athletic undergarments, the better to
stay cool, contained, and maneuverable.)

GINA: Where are the garbage bags?

STANLEY: Oh, shoot. I left them upstairs.

GINA: Seriously? Go get them.

STANLEY: (*Indicating his state of undress*) Like this?

GINA: Yano is at a friend's house until six. Nobody's
home.

STANLEY: Where are they?

GINA: Under the sink.

(STANLEY *begins to hurry up the stairs.*)

GINA: Honey? Get me some clothes?

STANLEY: Sure.

(STANLEY *hurries back out the door they came in.* GINA
begins gathering all the armor into a pile in front of the
couch. He comes back in, holding a box of big black lawn
garbage bags and a handful of clothes for her. He hurries
back down the steps and hands both to her.)

STANLEY: Bags. Clothes.

GINA: Thank you!

(GINA *rips two bags out of the box and hands one to* STANLEY. *They each start bagging up the discarded pieces of their armor.*)

STANLEY: I still say we burn them.

GINA: They're made of fiberglass and leather. Good luck burning that down to ash. It's killing me enough to get rid of them.

STANLEY: Gina…

GINA: Maybe we could just store them—

STANLEY: Gina!

GINA: I know.

(GINA *hands him her garbage bag.* STANLEY *hurries up the steps with both bags in tow, stops halfway.*)

STANLEY: Are we just ditching the bags, or—

GINA: The whole car. I think we have to.

STANLEY: Me too.

(STANLEY *hurries out the door.* GINA *pulls on the clothes he brought her: sweatpants, a T-shirt, slippers. She picks up her smartphone from a table next to the couch and begins scrolling through feeds. At the same time, she picks up the TV remote and flicks on the TV. The volume is low. Keeping one eye on her phone the whole time, she flips through channels on the television.*)

(STANLEY *re-enters. He no longer has the garbage bags, and he now wears basketball shorts, a t-shirt, and flip-flops. He, too, is looking at a smartphone.*)

STANLEY: I'm not seeing anything. Are you seeing anything?

GINA: No. Nothing on the news, either.

STANLEY: The news. They're at least an hour behind social media, and that's on the big stories.

GINA: This isn't a big story?

STANLEY: I mean, like, war and stuff.

GINA: *(Off of her phone)* I swear to God, I don't see a thing.

STANLEY: Is it possible nobody's noticed? Are you searching the right hashtags?

(GINA and STANLEY both dive back into their phones.)

GINA: Hashtag *Space Corps*: nothing.

STANLEY: Hashtag Pasadena Comic Con: nothing.

GINA: Hashtag Bruce Glover. Look!

(GINA shows STANLEY her phone. He reads:)

STANLEY: "Sitting here waiting for the hashtag Bruce Glover panel to begin. It's half an hour late. Double-you tee eff?"

(GINA and STANLEY look at each other, eyes wide.)

GINA: It's starting!

STANLEY: We did it.

GINA: Omigod omigod omigod…

STANLEY: Steady.

GINA: I can't believe we did it.

STANLEY: Steady!

GINA: I can't believe we did THAT.

STANLEY: We did that. WE did that.

GINA: Let's talk through it again. I'm starting to get anxious.

STANLEY: Gina.

GINA: Please.

STANLEY: Fine. The car's in the garage, so it's off the road. Armor's in the trunk. When it gets dark, we'll take it up to the lake and dump the whole thing.

GINA: The door to upstairs is triple-locked, the bathroom is up and running, shower stand and toilet and all.

STANLEY: Correct.

GINA: There are fresh linens for the fold-out couch on the shelf in the bathroom. Snacks and water are in the mini-fridge.

STANLEY: Should we unbind him?

GINA: Maybe. Did you take his mask off?

STANLEY: *(Realizing)* Oh, no!

GINA: That's the prop-accurate mask! Without the latex and the plastic tubes it's almost impossible to breathe in.

(STANLEY *hurries to the boiler room door and goes in.*)

GINA: How could you do that?

Stanley *(OS)* I just forgot.

GINA: We should have used the Halloween mask.

Stanley *(OS)* Ugh, a cheap costume store mask? We've got standards, Gina.

(STANLEY *reappears, dragging the half-conscious man in a Kookoochik costume out of the closet with him, dumping him on the couch, and then pulling the mask off of him. Revealed is* BRUCE GLOVER, *a 50-something year old man with a neatly trimmed salt-and-pepper beard. He is still.*)

GINA: Mr Glover! Mr Glover! Can you hear me? Mr Glover!

(BRUCE *coughs and sputters.* STANLEY *pushes him into a seating position and pats him on the back.*)

STANLEY: You're okay. It's okay. The mask had no breathing tubes. That's on me. Sorry.

(BRUCE's *coughing is dying out. He holds up his hand to indicate that he's fine. He clears his throat a few times, testing his airway...and then he lunges and tackles* STANLEY *to the floor, choking him.*)

GINA: Hey! Hey! Get off of him!

(GINA *tries to pull* BRUCE *off of* STANLEY *but he's locked on too tightly. She turns and picks up one of the replica rifles she and* STANLEY *had been armed with. She runs back over to the scuffling pair of men, raises the butt of the replica rifle high, and clocks* BRUCE *in the head with it, knocking him cold and into a...*)

(Blackout)

Interlude #1

(Spot up DSR where a news anchor, RICK HERNANDEZ, *sits at a desk, mid-report.)*

RICK HERNANDEZ: ...we are now able to confirm that filmmaker Bruce Glover has gone missing. The man behind the multi-billion dollar *Space Corps* film franchise was scheduled to speak on a panel this afternoon at the Pasadena Comic Book Convention. Although witnesses placed him at the convention earlier in the day, Mr Glover failed to arrive for that engagement. We go back to Natalie Crane on the scene. Natalie, what's the latest?

(Spot up DSL where an entertainment reporter, NATALIE CRANE, *is reporting from the scene.)*

NATALIE CRANE: Thanks, Rick. What we're now hearing is that Mr Glover had excused himself to use the restroom prior to speaking, and as far as can be gathered this was the last time anyone involved with

Pasadena Con spoke to him. Police are on the scene but their search is slow going.

RICK HERNANDEZ: And why is that, Natalie?

NATALIE CRANE: Attendees at these conventions often wear wild and elaborate costumes in a practice known as "cosplay". So what I'm hearing from my contacts in the convention center is that the police and the federal investigators who are also now on the scene are slowly evacuating the building, and they have to search each costumed attendee one-by-one in order to confirm their identities while they look for any leads to Mr Glover's whereabouts. As you can imagine, this process is… you know, it's inefficient.

RICK HERNANDEZ: Boy, sure sounds like it. *(Turns to camera)* That's the word from our pop culture correspondent, Natalie Crane. Thank you, Natalie, and be sure to keep us abreast of any updates.

NATALIE CRANE: Absolutely. I'll be here.

(Blackout)

(And then, from the darkness:)

GINA: Time to wake up, Mr Glover.

Scene 2

(Lights up)

(We're back in the basement. BRUCE, still in the Kookoochik costume but unmasked, is duct-taped to a rolling office chair. STANLEY stands behind him, GINA is in front of him, leaning over him.)

GINA: Can you hear me? Mr Glover!

(BRUCE begins to stir. He straightens up with a gasp of rusted pain, then looks around.)

GINA: How are you feeling?

(BRUCE *pulls against the duct tape strapping him to the chair.*)

BRUCE: I can't move!

STANLEY: That's just the duct tape.

GINA: How's your head?

BRUCE: It feels like a crushed canteloupe.

GINA: Sorry. You were a little upset, so I had to smack you in the head with the butt-end of a TS-620 rapid-repeat blaster rifle prop-accurate replica.

BRUCE: A what?

GINA: A TS-620 rapid-repeat blaster rifle prop-accurate replica.

(BRUCE, *still a little out of it, stares blankly at her.*)

GINA: A TS-620? Cheezits, you should know what it is; you invented it.

STANLEY: It's a limited edition. Killed us to take it out of the box but I really needed it for my convention cosplay.

GINA: Would you believe your skull dented the outer casing?

BRUCE: Who the hell are you people?!

GINA: My name is Gina, and this is my husband, Stanley.

STANLEY: We are big fans.

GINA: The biggest.

STANLEY: Huge. Our wedding was *Space Corps*-themed.

GINA: A seamstress friend made me a dress just like the one Princess Mia wore at the end of *Space Corps: Chapter 3*, with the starburst pattern and the big open sleeves?

STANLEY: She looked gorgeous.

GINA: We can show you pictures. Honey, can you get the wedding album? It's in our bedroom. My bookshelf, on the right. While you're up there also get—

BRUCE: *(Shouting)* Are you fucking kidding me?!

GINA: Excuse me?

BRUCE: Your wedding album?! What the fuck is wrong with you? What is going on here? Untie me, you assholes!

STANLEY: Wow. Okay. Well, I don't want to seem too old-fashioned or anything, but I just... you know, I just can't have you talking to my wife like that.

(STANLEY crosses to BRUCE, rears back, and slugs him across the face.)

BRUCE: Mother fucker!

STANLEY: Geez, did that hurt? It looked like it hurt.

GINA: I can get you some ice.

BRUCE: What the fuck is happening? I was taking a leak in the bathroom at the convention center, and then...

STANLEY: I hit you in the back of the head. Fun fact, I clocked you at the convention with the same TS-620 rapid-repeat blaster rifle prop-accurate replica that Gina hit you with just a minute ago.

GINA: You passed out right there in the bathroom and we put you into the Kaszuba costume and just carried you right out. You must have woken up in the trunk of our car on the way here, kind of? You were still pretty groggy when we pulled you out and walked you down into the basement.

BRUCE: You carried me out of the bathroom and nobody stopped you?

GINA: Only for pictures.

STANLEY: Everyone thought we were re-enacting the scene from *Space Corps: Chapter 2* where Link Cloudbringer and Yano Deuce dress up as Corps Fighters and sneak an unconscious Kaszuba the Kookoochik off of the Dead Sun warmonger satellite.

GINA: People were taking a TON of selfies with us. Cheering for us and everything. It was an all-time great Con moment.

BRUCE: Listen. I have money. Lots of money. Whatever you want, however much you need. Just name your price.

GINA: This is what we want.

STANLEY: You. Right here. Going nowhere.

BRUCE: What?

GINA: Mr Glover, my husband and I: we really love *Space Corps*.

STANLEY: We do. We love it so much.

GINA: It's not just a movie to us. It's spiritual. It's communal.

STANLEY: Our entire social network revolves around *Space Corps*, online and offline.

GINA: All of our best friends are Corpsmen and women.

STANLEY: We know the guy who made the winning short film at last year's *Space Corps* FanFest. I even helped him with the sound editing, a little.

GINA: We love *Space Corps*, and we are willing to do anything for it.

STANLEY: Anything.

GINA: So don't take this personally, Mr Glover.

STANLEY: It's just business.

BRUCE: You love my movies… so you kidnapped me?

GINA: Exactly.

BRUCE: Shoved me into a Kaszuba costume and hit me over the head with a…what was it again?

GINA: A TS-620 rapid-repeat—

BRUCE: I don't give a fuck what it was! Why am I here? You don't want me going anywhere? What does that even mean? Look. You're big fans. So you know what next week is.

GINA: Of course. God, who doesn't?

STANLEY: *Space Corps: Chapter 6* goes into production next week. That's why you were at Pasadena Con. Your last big pow-wow with the fans before going radio silent for the next two years to get the film made.

BRUCE: Exactly. Next week I start making the next *Space Corps* movie. Except, if I'm here? I can't DO that!

GINA: Right.

BRUCE: So I won't get to make it.

STANLEY: Right.

BRUCE: So you won't get to see it.

GINA: Exactly.

BRUCE: WELL WHAT THE FUCK?!

GINA: Mr Glover, keeping you from making that movie is kind of the whole point of this.

BRUCE: Excuse me?

STANLEY: This isn't easy for me to say, Mr Glover, but the last two *Space Corps* movies were, and I don't want to seem overdramatic here, but…they were flaming piles of kiddie nonsense garbage crap.

GINA: You gave the world such a gift, Mr Glover. But all gifts fade, in time. Your current vision of *Space Corps* just isn't the *Space Corps* we real fans wanted *Space Corps* to become. This is why my hubby and I have taken it upon ourselves to make sure that you, Bruce Glover, don't ever make another *Space Corps* movie for as long as you live.

BRUCE: Is this a joke? Is this for real? This isn't for real. Sherman must be behind this.

GINA: Who?

BRUCE: Sherman Schneider. The director.

STANLEY: Uh, I THINK we know who Sherman Schneider is.

GINA: God, famous people are friends with other famous people. That's so cool.

BRUCE: We've been pranking each other for decades. *(Calling out)* Okay, Sherman, I'm giving you this one! You got me! You can come out now.

(Sherman does not emerge, for Sherman is not there.)

BRUCE: *(Getting nervous)* Sherman? Come on. It's over, Sherm. I know this isn't real.

(GINA steps over to him and hits him hard across the face.)

GINA: Did that feel real?

BRUCE: Goddammit!

GINA: Mr Glover, between now and the time that they make a *Space Corps* movie without you…

STANLEY: …and they will; a little missing persons case isn't going to keep your studio from another billion dollar payday…

GINA: Between now and the time that movie comes out, at least, you are going to be a guest in our home.

BRUCE: But that could be years from now!

GINA: It could be. Which is why it is so, so important that you answer this next question honestly: is it too drafty down here for you? Do you want two blankets or do you think one will be fine?

(No response. BRUCE is horrified.)

GINA: You just think that over and let me know.

(GINA and STANLEY head for the stairs.)

STANLEY: Pot roast for dinner. Hope you're hungry.

GINA: Oooo, my hubby makes a mean pot roast! I'll bring some down to you in a few hours. You just make sure to have your appetite ready.

(GINA and STANLEY have reached the top of the steps. They look down at BRUCE.)

GINA: Mr Glover, please, believe us: this is for the best.

(GINA and STANLEY exit through the door. They slam it behind them. From the other side, they meticulously lock the door in three different places.)

(For several long moments, BRUCE sits in his chair, still duct-taped, still shell-shocked. He looks around, and then, one more time, out of agonizing desperation...)

BRUCE: *(Desperate)* Sherman?

(But SHERMAN is not there.)

(Blackout)

Interlude #2

(Spot up DSL. The Pasadena POLICE COMMISSIONER stands at a podium fielding questions from reporters.)

POLICE COMMISSIONER: ...Yes, go ahead.

(Spot up DSR on NATALIE CRANE, on holding a handheld microphone.)

NATALIE CRANE: Natalie Crane, WLAX Nightly News. Commissioner, can you confirm what you just said: there have been no leads, no ransom demands, no body, and no contact with any alleged abductors or suspects?

POLICE COMMISSIONER: I didn't say that.

NATALIE CRANE: …You said no arrests have been made or are impending, you've not been contacted by any--

POLICE COMMISSIONER: Now…now…wait. Just because we've not yet…uh…had initiated to us any direct contact from any alleged suspects doesn't mean we've not spoken to several persons of interest.

NATALIE CRANE: Have any of these persons of interest led to any sort of a lead?

POLICE COMMISSIONER: Again, this investigation is ongoing, so I'm not at liberty to get into those specifics.

NATALIE CRANE: Have you reached out to either of Mr Glover's ex-wives, and are they being considered persons of interest?

POLICE COMMISSIONER: Ah…no. Yes, we've reached out, but neither is a person of interest at this time. One was in Hawaii on her honeymoon at the time Mr Glover is reported to have gone missing, and as some in the media have noted she and Mr Glover have long-standing restraining orders out against each other since going through a contentious divorce. As we understand it they haven't seen each other in nearly a decade. His other ex-wife is now, as you may know, the First Lady of Ecuador, and was attending a public event in their capital city of Quito at the time Mr Glover went missing.

(Another reporter, JEB DUTT, dressed ultra-casually and a little bit slovenly in all Space Corps-themed gear, enters. In lieu of a microphone he speaks into a smartphone recorder.)

JEB DUTT: Jeb Dutt, Space Corpsmen Central-dot-com, at-SpaceCorpsmenCentral on Flitter. Commissioner, is it fair to assume that even if Mr Glover is never heard from again, GloverFilm will continue to make *Space Corps* movies?

POLICE COMMISSIONER: I really couldn't say, and this feels inappropriate—

JEB DUTT: If a *Space Corps* movie directed by anyone other than Bruce Glover is announced, wouldn't you line up to see it right now? Bruce had lost the thread of the series, after all. Due respect to the dead.

POLICE COMMISSIONER: He's not— We don't know if— How did you get cleared for this press event? Okay, we're done here. Thank you.

(The POLICE COMMISSIONER *leaves the podium and exits DSL.* NATALIE CRANE *exits DSR, giving* JEB DUTT *wide berth as he continues to shout out:)*

JEB DUTT: It's sad about Bruce, but the thing really at stake here is *Space Corps*, commissioner! It's *Space Corps*!

(Blackout)

Scene 3

(The basement. An un-duct taped BRUCE *sits on the couch. He has a black eye and a bandaged arm. His beard is starting to grow out.)*

(Next to him sits a TV tray, upon which is a plate with an uneaten sandwich. He wears sweats, slippers, and a bathrobe. The couch is a disarray of blankets and pillows.)

(The door opens. GINA *and* STANLEY *enter. She carries a tray with* BRUCE's *dinner on it.)*

GINA: Evening, Bruce!

STANLEY: Hey, buddy, how's your day been?

(BRUCE *does not respond. He does not even move. He simply stares straight ahead.*)

GINA: You're still not going to talk to us? Not even a hello?

(GINA *has reached* BRUCE'*s couch. She looks at his uneaten sandwich and shakes her head.*)

GINA: You haven't touched your lunch. Bruce, you must be hungry. You've been here three weeks. You have to eat. (*She places the dinner tray down next to* BRUCE'*s sandwich. She lifts the lid off of the dinner tray.*) Chicken. You like? It's my lemon pepper.

STANLEY: Best lemon pepper chicken in southeastern Pasadena.

GINA: (*Pleasantly embarrassed*) Oh, Stanley, stop it.

(BRUCE *doesn't respond.* GINA *sighs and sits next to him.*)

GINA: Bruce. We've been over this. We do not want you to die.

STANLEY: It would be a heck of a bother.

GINA: When you try and break our reinforced display cases and sprain your wrist, or take a swing at Stanley and end up with a black eye, you're only hurting yourself.

BRUCE: (*Mumbling*) Please tell me what you want from me.

STANLEY: What was that, Bruce? You're a little croaky.

GINA: You at least need to drink some water.

BRUCE: (*Louder*) What is it you want from me? Money? Memorabilia? A walk-on in *Chapter 6*? What is it that you really want?

STANLEY: Literally nothing.

BRUCE: That can't be true. You can't really be holding me here just to keep me from making anymore *Space Corps* movies.

GINA: That is what we told you and that is what it is.

BRUCE: I don't understand. You two love *Space Corps*. I have eyes, I can see what you have down here, all the props, the posters, the action figures. I'll bet the rest of your home is decorated the same.

STANLEY: It's true. This is just where we keep the spillover from the actual collection.

BRUCE: If you keep me here, there's not going to be any more of those things. *Space Corps* will be over. No more films, no more collectibles! I'm the only one who knows the whole story! It's my universe and my baby! They'd never make one without me!

GINA: You know how much money your franchise is worth, right?

BRUCE: Do you know how much money I'M worth? Do you have any idea how wealthy I could make you? You let me go now, and this is water under the bridge. I hear you. You're upset. You don't like some of the choices I've made. I get the message.

STANLEY: You said that after *Chapter 4*. And then you made *Chapter 5*, proving yourself a liar. No offense.

BRUCE: Offense taken.

STANLEY: Well, you know, suit yourself.

BRUCE: Think of what I'm offering you! A blank check! My personal assurance that the next *Space Corps* will be different! If you keep holding me here, though, you get nothing. When you get caught, and you will, you will get nothing!

STANLEY: We won't get caught.

BRUCE: The hell you won't! They're going to look at the security tapes from the convention, and they'll see two Corps Fighters enter the bathroom without a Kookoochik and leave the bathroom WITH a Kookoochik! You think that's not going to stand out as unusual to anyone?

GINA: It would...except when we walked into the convention we were already carrying a Kookoochik.

STANLEY: And we walked around with it for over an hour BEFORE going into the bathroom.

GINA: We filled the costume with balled-up paper towels so people would see us carrying it around before we put you in it. In the bathroom we emptied out the towels, threw them in the trash, waited for you to show up, and then knocked you out and stuffed you into the suit.

STANLEY: Which, believe us, was no easy thing. You ever try to stuff an unconscious man into a full-body carpet?

BRUCE: What about the bathroom security camera? They must have caught the whole assault on tape!

STANLEY: It wasn't working.

BRUCE: How do you know?

STANLEY: Because last month I went to a boat show at the convention center, and while I was there I unplugged the camera in the bathroom closest to Conference Hall 42, where we knew you'd be scheduled to speak.

GINA: It's where you're always scheduled to speak.

BRUCE: How'd you know I'd use the bathroom?

GINA: It's well known that you always go pee right before you give a talk. You get nervous.

BRUCE: That's well known?

GINA: Well, we knew.

BRUCE: And how do you know they haven't plugged the camera back in since that boat show?

STANLEY: Because the day we grabbed you the plug was still dangling down from the back of the camera.

BRUCE: When did you say this boat show was?

STANLEY: A month ago.

GINA: Six weeks, really.

BRUCE: Six weeks? I call bullshit. Why in the hell wouldn't the convention center people plug the camera back in at some point over six weeks?

STANLEY: It was in a men's bathroom, Bruce. They don't care. Men don't get assaulted in public bathrooms. If it was the ladies' room they'd have plugged it back in. Besides, those cameras are high up, maintenance would have had to drag a stepladder in there…what a pain. I had to wear stilts to reach it.

BRUCE: You wore stilts?

STANLEY: Yeah, it was part of my cosplay.

BRUCE: You cosplayed at the boat show?

STANLEY: I went as a lifeguard chair.

GINA: It's a great costume.

STANLEY: You want to see it?

BRUCE: …Kind of, yeah. (*Shakes his head*) No! No, I don't want to see it! Why would you go to all that trouble just to kidnap me and leave me here to rot?! How could you be that mad about chapters 4 and 5?

STANLEY: This may come as a surprise to you, Bruce, but *Space Corps* matters a lot to some people. Watching a *Space Corps* movie for the first time can be transformative. Can I tell you a story?

BRUCE: Let's not pretend I have a choice.

STANLEY: Yeah, good point. I'm going to tell you a story. When I was a kid, I was a bully.

BRUCE: I believe you.

STANLEY: I would get into fights, beat other kids up, steal their stuff. I didn't have much so I took from the kids who did. But then, when I was ten years old, I saw *Space Corps: Chapter 1—The Pirate's Apprentice*. On that screen in the dark, I saw a boy not much older than me with even less in his life than I had. Link Cloudbringer, the Pirate's Apprentice. Link risked everything to save Princess Mia and the Underground Renegades even though he was a slave, with nothing to gain for his good deed but a sonic lashing at the hands of his master, the dread pirate Blackheart. Meanwhile, I was wasting my life away fighting for dimes and nickels in the schoolyard and stealing soda pop from the corner store.

BRUCE: You're laying it on a little thick, Stan.

STANLEY: That movie changed me, Bruce. It showed me the error of my ways. It showed me how to be a good person.

BRUCE: Did it, though?

GINA: I was eight.

BRUCE: Oh, good, it's your turn.

GINA: I had a little kitchen set in my bedroom. I pretended I was making dinner while my brothers played at being ninjas and superheroes. They were learning they could be anything beyond their wildest imagination. I was learning that I could be my mother. So when I saw *The Pirate's Apprentice*, and I saw Princess Mia carrying around a lazer cannon and blasting away at Corps Fighters while ordering her generals around…it set me free. It told me that I could be anything I wanted to be. I didn't need to spend my life chained to a Frigidaire and an oven.

STANLEY: And then there was the guy we both loved: Yano Deuce.

GINA: The once-celebrated Corpsman who sees through the Solar Monarch's facade, and then turns on his former brothers-in-arms with nobody at his side but the mighty Kaszuba.

BRUCE: Is that what this is? You two are Yano purists?

GINA: Is there any other way to be?

BRUCE: Listen. Addison Dodge was a starving actor almost out of the biz back then. He was working as a plumber to make his rent. He'd have taken any role I offered and he'd have been grateful for it. Now he's one of the biggest stars in Hollywood. He wouldn't sign on for *Chapter 4* unless I made Yano the bad guy.

STANLEY: You should have found another way. Yano Deuce, the villain of *Chapter 4*? It makes no sense. He'd never have betrayed Link and Mia.

BRUCE: Yeah, well, when "Yano Deuce" threatened to walk off the production after my first draft of the *Chapter 4* script violated, in his lawyer's words, "The spirit of the agreed-upon direction of Mr Dodge's character?" That's when I started to believe that Yano Deuce could turn to evil. Necessity is the mother of invention. It wasn't my first choice, but I made it work.

STANLEY: You didn't.

BRUCE: Okay, Stanley, we'll agree to disagree.

STANLEY: No. You didn't make it work. You betrayed your fans. Better you had recast the role.

BRUCE: *(Guffaws)* Can you imagine the reaction on social media if I had recast Addison Dodge? Jesus, you people are the same fans who went apeshit when I did the *Space Corps 1 Enhanced Edition*.

STANLEY: You changed the movie!

BRUCE: I tweaked the movie. A tiny bit. I made it prettier.

GINA: You had the Monarch swing first!

BRUCE: It works better that way, for character. In the original version, Yano is standing there in the throne room renouncing his Corpsman status, and out of nowhere he whips out a photon axe and swings for the Monarch's head. In the updated version the Monarch swings first with a sun disc, and it looks like Yano was acting out of self defense. It works.

(STANLEY *backhands* BRUCE *across the face.*)

STANLEY: It does NOT work! Who do you think you are, changing our movies like that?

(BRUCE *shakily pushes himself back up, one hand pressed against his cheek where* STANLEY *struck him.*)

BRUCE: Fuck you, Stanley. YOUR movies? They are MY movies, you son of a bitch!

(STANLEY *rears back to hit* BRUCE *again, but this time* BRUCE *is ready. He catches* STANLEY's *arm and holds it. The two men get tangled together and end up scuffling on the floor.*)

(GINA *calmly crosses over to the display case, takes out a key ring, and unlocks it. She withdraws a rod that she extends to two feet long with a snap of her wrist. She walks over to the two wrestling men.*)

GINA: Stanley?

(STANLEY *quickly extricates himself from the fight, and* GINA *jabs* BRUCE *with the end of the rod.* BRUCE *jumps like he's just been jolted with a large shock of electricity... probably because he has just been jolted with a large shock of electricity. As* BRUCE *quivers on the ground,* GINA *retracts the rod and hands it to* STANLEY, *who returns it to the display case.)*

GINA: Can you also imagine, Bruce, how upset I was when in *Space Corps: Chapter 4—Black Shadows Fall,* Princess Mia's role was reduced to pleading with her husband to go save their child? The Mia I knew would have jumped into a warp pod and gone off to find her daughter on her own. Instead she stays behind in the palace, wearing heavy gowns and weeping.

(BRUCE *is still on the ground, recovering from the shock.)*

BRUCE: *(Gasping)* What the fuck was that?

GINA: A shock-rod.

BRUCE: You have a working shock rod?

GINA: Any self-respecting fan has a working shock rod. Come on.

(GINA *and* STANLEY *help* BRUCE *to the couch.)*

GINA: Should we talk now about Ding-Dong Diggum?

BRUCE: Please no.

GINA: We should talk about Ding-Dong Diggum.

BRUCE: Oh god.

GINA: You stand by Yano Deuce going evil, you stand by the Solar Monarch swinging first…do you stand by Ding-Dong Diggum?

STANLEY: A completely digital character who talks with a racist accent and is the butt of several fart jokes. In a *Space Corps* movie.

BRUCE: He is a hero kidnapper trying to protect Link and Mia's daughter from the now treacherous Yano…

GINA: You named him Ding-Dong Diggum, and he hops around spouting off with nonsense like, "Berry

berry good, little princess. Ding-Dong get de gassy when he nervous!"

STANLEY: Holy shit.

GINA: "Oh, yah, little princess! Ding-Dong eat'em the yum yum goodies!"

STANLEY: And the walk. My God, the walk.

(STANLEY *demonstrates Ding-Dong's stupid walk.*)

STANLEY: "You a berry, berry bad man, Yano Douche, you a berry, berry bad man." Maybe we SHOULD kill you.

BRUCE: Ding-Dong isn't for you two, okay? I made Ding-Dong for the kids. The kids love him. He tested really well with the kids.

STANLEY: Whose dumbass kids were those?

BRUCE: I'm making family films here.

GINA: There is a difference between "family-films" and flat-out childish.

STANLEY: When it was announced that *Chapter 4* was finally getting made after ten long years of no *Space Corps* movies, we swore we were going to see it at least a dozen times in the theater. We were so disappointed by it, do you know how many times we ended up seeing it? Six. Only six times.

GINA: And then *Chapter 5* was even WORSE than *Chapter 4*: more Ding-Dong, more evil Yano, hackneyed love story… that is when we realized something had to be done. So. We did it. *(Beat)* I think this was good. We cleared the air. This will help make the coming days less awkward.

BRUCE: You two are insane.

GINA: No. We just believe in *Space Corps*. Even if you no longer do.

BRUCE: But I do.

STANLEY: Liar. If you still believed in *Space Corps* as the fans do? You never, ever would have dared to go back and change our movies. That may really have been your biggest sin of all, in my eyes. Yano swung first, Bruce. Period. Yano. Swung. First.

GINA: Eat your dinner, Bruce.

(GINA *clears the sandwich away and leaves the dinner; she and* STANLEY *start up the steps.*)

BRUCE: (*Calling after them*) "Art is never finished, only abandoned."

(GINA *and* STANLEY *stop and look down at* BRUCE.)

BRUCE: I think DaVinci said that. Someone said it. *Chapter 1* wasn't finished when I put it out. In those days I had a film degree, a well-received indie film, and a crazy idea for a space opera that nobody wanted to finance. I had to pay for the film myself with credit cards, and I had maxed them all out before I ran out of script. Half of the special effects I invented, and the other half I fudged. It was a polished turd of a movie, but I got it out onto a handful of screens and it took off. In spite of its shortcomings, people loved it. It made me a very wealthy man, yes, but I'm an artist, and when I looked back on this thing that defined my career I saw the flaws I couldn't afford to fix the first time around. Once I had the means, I went back to *Chapter 1* and fixed the unfinished parts of it that I had always hated. That is my right. It is mine. I made it. I paid for it. I own it. I market it. I took all of the risk. *The Space Corps 1: Enhanced Edition* made millions of dollars. The blemishes were removed. Why does its existence make you so angry?

GINA: When an artist puts art out into the world they've given it up for adoption. You may have created

Space Corps, but it belongs to all of us now, and we loved it as it was. You don't love something in spite of its flaws, Bruce. You love something unconditionally, flaws and all. You take the flaws away, and suddenly that thing is no longer the thing you loved. You really can't see that?

STANLEY: They're not going to find you, Bruce. You should eat some chicken. It's really, really good.

(GINA *and* STANLEY *ascend the stairs, still talking with each other.)*

GINA: You're gonna make me blush.

STANLEY: Well, it is. It's the best.

GINA: YOU'RE the best.

STANLEY: Ooo, I'll show YOU the best...

GINA: *(Giggling)* Stop it!

(GINA *and* STANLEY *go through door at the top of the stairs, slamming it shut behind them. Several locks click shut. Miserably,* BRUCE *begins to eat his chicken.)*

BRUCE: That is pretty good chicken.

(Blackout)

Interlude #3

(Spot up DSR. RICK HERNANDEZ *sits at his news desk.)*

RICK HERNANDEZ: It has been almost nine months now, and the search for Bruce Glover is losing steam and hope. Today, in what could be described as a Hail Mary pass, Oscar-winning filmmaker Sherman Schneider made a statement on his closest friend's behalf.

(A spot comes up on SHERMAN SCHNEIDER, *standing at a downstage podium, several news microphones in front of*

him, flashbulbs going off intermittently. He reads from a prepared statement.)

SHERMAN: *(Reading)* "I know in my heart that my dear friend Bruce is still out there, but I don't know why he has been taken from us. I have woken up every morning over these past nine months with renewed hope that this will be the day Bruce comes home. Bruce, if you went away on your own, I beg of you: just let us know. Send us a sign we can believe. If you wanted to remove yourself from the public eye, we, those of us who love you, would understand. We just need to know that you are okay. If something more untoward happened, if Bruce has been taken, and for what purpose I can't imagine, I speak now to his abductors: you have stolen from us all a keeper of imagination and a builder of worlds. Humanity is better when Bruce Glover and his vision for *Space Corps* is a part of it. Taking our dreamers away hurts us all. Bruce Glover is a gift to the citizens of this planet. Please, I'm begging you, in the words of Bruce's most famous character, Link Cloudbringer: 'May the Light shine his way home.' Thank you."

(Flashbulbs go off as SHERMAN leaves the podium.

(Blackout)

Scene 4

(The basement. BRUCE sits on the sofa. His beard is really starting to get out of control. GINA stands atop the staircase. She is holding the photo albums.)

BRUCE: Down here alone? No Stan the Man to watch your back?

GINA: Stanley's out to the toy store with Yano.

BRUCE: *(Shaking his head)* I still can't believe you named your son after Yano Deuce. That poor kid.

GINA: You're the one who came up with it!

BRUCE: I picked it because it sounded like a weird-ass space name nobody in their right mind would give to their actual human child here on Earth. How was I supposed to know some superfans would someday want to scar their son for life by naming him first name Yano, middle name Deuce? It's slang for shit, you know that, right? You middle-named your son after dropping a number two. What do you want, anyway?

(GINA holds up the photo albums.)

GINA: I thought maybe while we were home alone, you'd finally look at the pictures.

BRUCE: Fuck you.

GINA: Yeah. Okay. *(She turns and heads towards the steps. She's almost to the top, when:)*

BRUCE: Wait.

(GINA stops and looks down.)

GINA: Yes?

(BRUCE is struggling. He doesn't want to give GINA the satisfaction...but he's been in the basement for nine months. He is super bored.)

BRUCE: I'll thumb through them. What the hell.

GINA: Yay! *(Excited, she descends the steps again. She stops on the bottom step and flicks open the shock-rod in her hand. Apologetically:)* Sorry. Just...

BRUCE: *(Sourly)* ...Just so we all know who's in charge. Sure.

(GINA crosses gingerly to behind the couch. Shock rod at the ready, she places the first of the two albums down next to BRUCE. He picks it up and begins to thumb through it.)

BRUCE: So these are of your wedding?

GINA: That one is.

BRUCE: Oh boy.

GINA: You like it?

BRUCE: Good ol' Stan dressed as Link Cloudbringer in his ceremonial garb...

GINA: ...and I wore an exact replica of Princess Mia's wedding gown from the end of *The Lost Paladin*.

BRUCE: *Chapter 3*, right. Did Stanley's groomsmen all dress up as Paladin Envoys?

GINA: Right down to the Sun-Swords.

BRUCE: And the bridesmaids are all wearing outfits Mia wears from across the first three films. *(Laughs)* Look at this one, in the assault armor from *Chapter 2*, complete with a lazer cannon. Good Lord.

GINA: That's my maid of honor. In the invitation we suggested our guests dress up as well. Most wore a t-shirt or something, but some of them went full cosplay. Our truest friends.

BRUCE: Is this guy dressed as—

GINA: —he's a Destroyer Bot, yes.

BRUCE: That costume must be the size of a small truck.

GINA: Mm-hmm. The whole thing barely fit through the door.

BRUCE: Look at that, *Space Corps* cake toppers.

GINA: *(Excitedly)* That's nothing. Turn the page, turn the page.

(BRUCE *does so.*)

BRUCE: Oh my.

GINA: All the food at the reception was modeled after food that's eaten in the background of the Luna Pub scene from *Pirate's Apprentice*. Minus the meteor grubs, of course. Stanley thought that might be a bridge too far. I thought eating potato croquettes shaped to look like big fat maggots would be amazing. No marriage is perfect, I guess.

(BRUCE *closes the album.*)

BRUCE: I've seen photos from *Space Corps*-themed weddings before, but I have to give it to you: this is certainly one of the more impressive I've ever come across.

GINA: Now look at this.

(*Shock-rod still armed,* GINA *hands* BRUCE *the second album from where she stands behind the couch. He opens it up. He gapes as he turns pages.*)

BRUCE: Is this…

GINA: *(Beaming)* It is.

BRUCE: This is a *Space Corps*-themed funeral.

GINA: It is!

BRUCE: You've got the pallbearers dressed up the same as the ones from the Queen's burial among the stars, the casket is an exact replica, even the attendees are in traditional Monarchy mourning garb. This is mind-blowing.

GINA: You've never seen a *Space Corps*-themed funeral before?

BRUCE: I have not.

GINA: They're not common, but they happen.

BRUCE: Whose funeral is it?

GINA: My mother's. It was just a few years back.

BRUCE: Oh. Um…my condolences.

GINA: Thank you.

BRUCE: Even though you're holding me prisoner in your basement.

GINA: That's big of you.

BRUCE: Don't push it. Your mother was a *Space Corps* fan, too?

GINA: Absolutely not. She hated it. Thought it was nonsense. Didn't understand why I was so devoted to a "bunch of silly movies". *(Adding quickly)* Her words, not mine.

BRUCE: So why'd you have a *Space Corps* funeral for her?

GINA: Because I wanted to. What was she going to do, stop me?

BRUCE: That would have been difficult.

GINA: Stanley actually didn't think it was a good idea. Once I put my foot down and it was happening he got into it because of course he did, but we argued over it. "There's limits", he said.

BRUCE: Are there? Limits, I mean.

GINA: No. There aren't. He made up that story, you know.

BRUCE: Which one?

GINA: About being a bully as a kid and *Space Corps* changing his life. He did see the movie as a kid, but when we first met he wasn't really... I don't know how to put this.

BRUCE: He wasn't really a fan?

GINA: They were movies that he liked, which is fine. When he and I started getting serious is when he really started deep-diving into the fandom.

BRUCE: For you.

GINA: Not FOR me, but…it's like the passion was there in him, but he needed something to ignite it.

BRUCE: Right. You. *(Chuckling)* That's funny.

GINA: What is?

BRUCE: Usually it's the girl who has to pretend to like *Space Corps* for the guy. Usually you don't see it the other way around. It's just funny.

GINA: A "girl" can't like *Space Corps*? We can't be real fans? Is that it? Because I'll tell you, I don't put up with that crap.

BRUCE: That's the farthest thing from what I meant. You are the personal living proof that women can be fans of my films just as much as men, but the demographics are what they are. Someone better versed in gender studies can explain why, whether its a natural difference in the sexes or if that's how society programs men and women to behave, that we've okayed it for men to like sci-fi and sports and for women to like, I don't know…flowers and dresses?

GINA: I'm starting to understand why you've been divorced twice.

BRUCE: Neither of my ex-wives understood that they'd never be the first thing on my mind. This is why Stanley makes a fine, loyal husband. You are the first thing on his mind. *Space Corps* is not. As I said: he is a pretender.

GINA: Stanley is not pretending to like *Space Corps*.

BRUCE: But his connection isn't to the art. It's to you. If we were to remove you from the equation, I bet he'd fade out of the fandom.

GINA: So he retconned his own past. So what? He gave himself a better fan origin story. It's who he decided he wanted to be.

BRUCE: No, he decided he wanted to be your husband.

(GINA *smiles.*)

GINA: Maybe. Honestly, he's been telling that bully story so long that he might even believe it by now.

BRUCE: Even though it's not true. Unlike your story, in which you decided that having a *Space Corps*-themed funeral for your mother was more important than saying good-bye to her in a manner she would have preferred.

GINA: Now you've got it.

BRUCE: And Stanley thought it was too much.

GINA: At first, but—

BRUCE: Then which of you am I to think is the bigger fan of my life's work?

(GINA *thinks that over.*)

GINA: I really did find the person that I am through *Space Corps*. That's why I had the funeral. I needed to say goodbye to my mother as my true self. To do it as anyone but the woman that *Space Corps* revealed me to be would have been…insincere.

BRUCE: I see.

GINA: You must think now that I'm even crazier than you thought I was before.

BRUCE: A little less, actually.

GINA: Oh. (*She smiles. She disarms the shock-rod.*) I'm glad.

(*Blackout*)

Interlude #4

(Spot up DSL. NATALIE CRANE *appears on location.)*

NATALIE CRANE: On the one-year anniversary of Bruce Glover's mysterious disappearance, a flurry of activity surrounds his namesake company. Venerable Hollywood heavyweight Wally Boys Pictures has acquired GloverFilm in a major media acquisition. Among other GloverFilm properties, Wally Boys adds to their studio portfolio the wildly popular *Space Corps* film franchise. Wally Boys is wasting no time, announcing just moments after the long-rumored sale became official that a new *Space Corps* film will be placed in immediate development, to be written and directed by Academy Award winning filmmaker and Bruce Glover's good friend, Sherman Schneider.

(Spot up on SHERMAN *DC, again at a news podium.)*

SHERMAN: I want to thank Wally Boys. This is truly an honor. This all came together so quickly, but I'm pretty sure... *(He chokes up.)* I'm pretty sure that this is what Bruce would have wanted. I'm going to do my best to make him proud of me, wherever he is. This is still so early in the process. I have some ideas, maybe an outline or two exists, I'm not giving anything away, no spoilers here!

(The press laughs. SHERMAN *does as well.)*

SHERMAN: Production will start in earnest next month, not until after the memorial service we're putting together for Bruce. That seems fitting. That seems right. After we pay our respects, we will continue on with the man's work. Thank you, no questions. *(He leaves the podium.)*

(Blackout)

Scene 5

(Lights up on the basement. BRUCE *sits on the folded-out sofa bed. His beard is really wild now.* GINA *and* STANLEY *stand behind him. They are watching TV. Orchestral music plays from out of the television.)*

BRUCE: *(Half-muttering)* Un-freaking-believable.

GINA: It's nice, though. The whole cast is there.

STANLEY: Michael Napier, Cassie Grail…even Addison Dodge. All things considered, that's a win, right?

BRUCE: I made them all rich and famous, the absolute least they could do for me was show up to my goddamn memorial service.

STANLEY: I'll bet this pulls a nice number. It's like a state funeral.

GINA: It really looks like you were loved. What a turnout.

BRUCE: *(Scoffing)* Loved? You think I was loved? You think these people loved me? Please.

*(*BRUCE *gets to his feet and starts anxiously pacing.* STANLEY *points to the TV.)*

STANLEY: Ooo, look, a twenty-one Sun-Sword salute.

GINA: I think Sherman Schneider is going to speak next.

*(*BRUCE *grabs the remote and clicks off the TV.)*

STANLEY: I get it. Watching your own funeral…that could be pretty unsettling.

GINA: Bruce? Are you okay?

*(*BRUCE *has slumped down against the wall, head in his hands.)*

STANLEY: Bruce? Buddy? You feeling all right?

GINA: Would you like some Pepto?

BRUCE: That's that. It's all over. They're putting me on the raft, pushing me out to the sea, and shooting the whole of it with a flaming arrow.

STANLEY: I think you're maybe overstating it.

BRUCE: They're eulogizing me as we speak. Eulogizing! I don't understand. It's just been a year. Why have they forgotten me so quickly? A year, in the grand scheme of things, isn't that long, is it? They don't even know for sure that I'm dead. They can't be sure, because I'm not. They'd rather have some big goddamn show than continue to look for me. They don't care about me at all, do they? Not a single one of them.

STANLEY: It's not that they don't care about you, Bruce. It's just they care less about you than they do about *Space Corps*.

GINA: *(Hissing)* Stanley! *(To* BRUCE*)* He didn't mean that.

BRUCE: *(Laughing)* Yes, he did. I'm not even mad. How can I be mad at that, when it's true?

STANLEY: It's not an insult! Isn't that the point of making art? To create something bigger than yourself?

BRUCE: You're right, Stanley. I hate it, and you, but you're right. The art outliving the artist, that's the goal. I just didn't think it'd come in the form of being kidnapped by crazy people and locked in a basement while the world buries me alive and steals my movies.

GINA: When you disappeared, GloverFilm stock cratered. Your shareholders had no choice but to sell out to Wally Boys. And GloverFilm only has value if *Space Corps* comes with it. A new *Space Corps* movie was always going to come sooner rather than later.

STANLEY: We tried to tell you that.

BRUCE: I didn't believe you. Who would want to? Who would want to acknowledge they're no longer needed to shepherd the thing they created?

STANLEY: Everyone knows who Superman is, Bruce, but most people couldn't tell you who came up with him.

(Awkward silence. Then, BRUCE begins to laugh. Slowly, at first, but building steam.)

GINA: Bruce? Are you okay?

STANLEY: Does that sound like an "okay" laugh to you? Get the shock-rod.

GINA: No! *(She crosses to BRUCE and kneels down next to him.)* Bruce, is there anything I can do?

BRUCE: *(Still laughing)* It's all so goddamned ridiculous, isn't it? But you two fucking nutbars must be thrilled. This is just what you wanted. I'll bet you're both pretty excited that my old buddy Sherman is going to make a new *Space Corps* movie.

STANLEY: Honestly? Heck, yeah! It's Sherman Schneider, three time Oscar winner!

BRUCE: Who couldn't kick me into my grave fast enough.

STANLEY: You're going to thank us when you see the film Sherman Schneider makes.

BRUCE: See it?! How?! Oh, Stanley, you're right, I can't wait for the home video release so down here in my eternal basement hideaway I can watch the gifted golden touch of God that my would-be best friend will have graced upon my shitburger magnum opus. I'm sorry that my hack-director's eye wasn't up to the standards that made you fall head-over-heels in love with *Space Corps* to begin with. But tell me this, Stan: if my movies are such shit that you'd commit a felony to keep me from making more of them, what does it say about you that you love them so much?

STANLEY: You're right. It makes no sense. I love *Space Corps*, with everything I have, even though they're obviously not, like, these great artistic films.

GINA: Of course they are. Stanley!

BRUCE: No, Gina, let him finish. Go on, Stanley, tell us more about how the movies you've given over your entire personal identity to are giant piles of steaming horse turds.

STANLEY: No! No. That's not…they are great movies. They are. What they AREN'T are great films, but they ARE great movies. Great, like, popcorn action movies, a little bit cliched and a little hacky, a little ham-fisted, but all in the best way, in a totally entertaining way! There's nothing wrong with a great movie; I love great movies. But a movie is just entertainment, right? A film, though, is art! So it'll be interesting to see, don't you think? It'll be interesting to see a *Space Corps* film made by an Academy Award winning director.

BRUCE: Right. Sure. I get it. Because he's Sherman Schneider.

STANLEY: Right.

BRUCE: He's won Oscars.

STANLEY: Yes.

BRUCE: And I'm just the schmuck who made *Space Corps*.

STANLEY: Yes. Wait. No. You're twisting this.

GINA: Is he?

STANLEY: Yes! Don't you start in on me now, this is exactly what we wanted. Bruce Glover away from *Space Corps*, and *Space Corps* in the hands of a great filmmaker, and we've got it. Our plan worked. It worked!

GINA: You don't have to be so rude about it.

BRUCE: Rude? Sweetie, you've kept me locked in your basement for a year. We are way past "rude". In fact, you know what? This isn't your basement anymore. It's mine. Get out, both of you.

(GINA *and* STANLEY *hesitate. She takes a breath to speak up, but…*)

BRUCE: Did you hear me? Get the fuck out of my basement! Get out! Get out! Get out!

(GINA *and* STANLEY *hurry up the steps.* GINA *stops.*)

GINA: I think you'll really be happy with the film Sherman ends up making.

BRUCE: Go fuck yourself.

(GINA *hurries out and closes the door behind her.*)

(*Blackout*)

Interlude #5

(*Spot up DSR.* NATALIE CRANE *is reporting live from outside of a local multiplex, where a line of rabid Space Corps fans have been lined up for days in anticipation of the premier of Space Corps: Chapter 6. Standing with NATALIE is an excited fan,* SEBASTIAN WATTS, *decked out in cosplay as Yano Deuce.*)

NATALIE CRANE: I'm here at Crown City Multiplex alongside a line of eager *Space Corps* fans, many in costume, some having been in line for, get this, a full week. I have one with me right now.

(NATALIE CRANE *turns to SEBASTIAN.*)

NATALIE CRANE: Sir, when did you get in line?

SEBASTIAN WATTS: Four days ago! Got a little grill
here, got my sleeping bag, my stuffed Kaszuba doll to
hold my spot in line while I run into the McDonalds to
pee… I'm ready! We're all ready!

(GINA's voice can be heard, echoing slightly.)

GINA: *(VO)* Yano…Yano? Yano, come on.

NATALIE CRANE: And who are you dressed as?

GINA: *(VO)* Yano, we're going to be late.

SEBASTIAN WATTS: My boy Yano Deuce, pre-*Pirate*
days. Yano swung first!

NATALIE CRANE: He certainly did. She turns back to the
camera.) As you can see, this crowd is beyond excited.

GINA: *(VO)* Stanley, have you seen Yano?

NATALIE CRANE: The first *Space Corps* movie in the
post-Bruce Glover era, *Chapter 6: A New Beginning*,
opens in just a few minutes. Now back to you in the
studio.

(Blackout)

(In the darkness…)

GINA: *(VO)* Hey, what is this? *(Alarmed)* Why is the
basement door open?!

Scene 6

*(Lights up on the basement. The door is open, and so is
the display case. BRUCE, facial hair grown out to Yeti-like
proportions by now, sits in a chair, his back to a wall so
nobody can get behind him. A boy of about ten years old
sits on his lap. BRUCE is holding a Pirate's Assassin Blade,
a replica he's sharpened to a razor edge, against the boy's
throat.)*

(This boy is YANO. He is GINA and STANLEY's son.)

(GINA *enters. She is in a Princess Mia Solaria costume. It is opening night for* Space Corps: Chapter 6, *and she has dressed accordingly.)*

(She sees the scene below her. She goes cold.)

GINA: No!

BRUCE: Hello, Gina. Stay right where you are and call for Stanley to come down here, would you?

(GINA is frozen, too scared to think, let alone move.)

BRUCE: Gina… *(He pushes the knife a little bit harder against YANO's throat.)* …call Stanley.

YANO: *(Scared)* Mommy!

GINA: Stanley! Stanley!

(STANLEY appears at the top of the steps. He's dressed as the Pirate King.)

STANLEY: Guys, we're gonna be late… *(He stops short, taking in the scene below him, realizing instantly that it's all over.)* Oh no.

BRUCE: If it makes the both of you feel any better, neither of you left the door open. A young boy's curiosity got the better of him and he came down on his own. He did, however, get too close.

STANLEY: Where did you get that knife?

BRUCE: You've had me locked down here for three years, Stanley. You think I wasn't teaching myself how to pick locks over all of that time? Didn't help me with the security door up there, but your display cases are mine for the taking.

STANLEY: That's just a prop knife.

BRUCE: I broke it out six months ago. Been sharpening it on loose slate back in the boiler room. You guys don't skimp on your replica props. High-quality steel

on this blade. Took the edge nicely. Now get your asses
down here. Keep your hands where I can see them.

(GINA *and* STANLEY *put their hands up and head slowly
down the steps.* BRUCE *tosses two pairs of Monarchy
Interrogation Binders to them.*)

BRUCE: Here. "Monarchy Interrogation Binders".
Another couple of prize replicas from your collection.
Lock yourselves to the radiator.

STANLEY: Bruce, let's talk about this. We can work
something out.

YANO: Daddy!

GINA: You can go, Bruce. Just let my son go, please.
Have us arrested, send us to jail, do whatever you like,
but let my son go!

STANLEY: Let's not be hasty, Gina.

GINA: It's our son, Stanley, for God's sake!

BRUCE: I like the way you're thinking, Gina. Priorities
still in order. Now, the both of you: get those goddamn
binders on.

(GINA *grabs a pair of binders and locks herself to the
radiator.* STANLEY *hesitates.*)

YANO: Daddy, please! He's hurting me, Daddy!

GINA: *(Screaming)* Goddammit, Stanley, get in those
fucking binders!

STANLEY: Okay! Okay! Here!

(STANLEY *grabs the other pair of binders and locks himself to
the radiator.*)

STANLEY: You happy now?

BRUCE: Tug on them.

(STANLEY *tugs on them. They're on good.*)

STANLEY: There.

BRUCE: Gina?

GINA: They're on tight.

BRUCE: Tug on the binders, Gina.

(GINA *does. They're secure.)*

GINA: *(Near tears)* See? Now, please, Bruce, please. We're so sorry. Please, please, let him go.

(BRUCE *shrugs.)*

BRUCE: Okay.

(YANO *hops off of* BRUCE'*s lap, runs over to his parents, and begins kicking them.)*

YANO: What the hell is wrong with you two?! You kidnapped Bruce Glover and you locked him in our basement?! Are you crazy?!

STANLEY: Ow! Yano! What are you doing?!

BRUCE: You told him the place was being fumigated? For three years? You had a silverfish infestation for three years? You managed to make me disappear without a trace and yet you couldn't think of a better lie to tell your own son?

YANO: God, I absolutely hate you both so much.

GINA: Yano! I don't understand.

BRUCE: He came down. He got nosy. Once he realized what had happened, and I got him to calm down, he was more than happy to let me out of here, so long as I helped him give you two a scare first. Spoiler alert: I was not hard to convince.

GINA: You mean you weren't going to—

BRUCE: —slit your son's throat? God, no. I'm not a monster. I'm not you two.

STANLEY: We aren't monsters.

YANO: You've kept a guy locked in our basement for three years because you didn't like some movies he made!

STANLEY: Yano, you know how bad *Chapters 4* and *5* were. We have talked about this.

YANO: Shut up! You never listen to me! I LIKED *Chapters 4* and *5*! All of my friends liked *Chapters 4* and *5*!

STANLEY: Your friends are dumb little shits!

YANO: And I like Ding-Dong Diggum! I think he's funny!

STANLEY: YOU ARE DEAD TO ME, YANO! YOU ARE NO SON OF MINE!

GINA: Stanley!

STANLEY: No son of mine likes Ding-Dong. NO SON OF MINE LIKES DING-DONG!

YANO: And the Sun Monarch swung first!

GINA: *(Scandalized)* Yano!

BRUCE: It is the strangest things that drive a gap between parents and their children.

YANO: What do we do now, Mr Glover?

BRUCE: Tell me, kid: you feel like taking in a movie?

YANO: Can we get popcorn with butter?

BRUCE: Normally I'd say that's bad for my cholesterol, but I've been trapped in a fucking basement for three years, so fuck it. We can even skip the popcorn and drink the butter straight, if you like. I don't give a shit.

YANO: Yeah!

BRUCE: Go get your coat.

(YANO gives both STANLEY and GINA one last kick apiece.)

YANO: That's for naming me Yano, you dicks. *(He runs upstairs.)*

BRUCE: Yeah, for that one? You guys are getting off light. Okay, see you later. *(He laughs)* That was a joke. I will not see you later.

(BRUCE exits up the stairs. GINA and STANLEY remain on the floor.)

STANLEY: To be fair, three years is way longer than we thought we'd be able to keep him prisoner.

GINA: Shut up, Stanley.

(Blackout)

END OF ACT ONE

ACT TWO

Prologue

(The Space Corps March *again blares to life. The deep voice* NARRATOR *speaks:)*

(Author's Note: Again, if there's any way this piece of narration can be scrolled up on a screen, go for it.)

NARRATOR: *(VO)* Disgust!

That's what courses through Bruce Glover's veins as he sits and watches *Space Corps: Chapter Six—A New Beginning,* directed by his longtime friend Sherman Schneider.

A distraught Bruce returns his young friend Yano, the son of his former abductors Stanley and Gina, back home before disappearing into the night. Rather than go to the police to turn Stanley and Gina in, Bruce finds himself wandering the streets of Pasadena, alone and enraged.

Unable to shake his anger over the lifeless, retread story told in A NEW BEGINNING, Bruce concludes that it is time for he and his old friend Sherman to have a little chat, but not on Sherman's terms. On Bruce's...

Scene 1

(Lights up)

(The door at the top of the stairs kicks open, and an odd procession marches in and down the steps. Two head-to-toe armored Corps Fighters [The foot soldiers of Space Corps' evil Solar Monarchy] come before and behind a captured Kookoochik [a sentient space bear], the Kookoochik's arms secured in binders. Fighter #1, standing in front, is leading the Kookoochik by a chain secured around its neck. Fighter #2 brings up the rear, and is holding a sci-fi blaster rifle, cockily swinging it around with one hand like he's in a stylish kung-fun movie.)

(The Corps Fighters march the Kookoochik, who is wobbly as he goes, down the steps and towards the door under the stairs.)

(They stop in front of the boiler room door. Fighter #2, STANLEY, raps three times on the door sharply and then calls through it to someone on the other side.)

STANLEY: We're back.

(STANLEY and GINA [in the other suit of armor] march the Kookoochik to the couch and force him down by the shoulders.)

(GINA points at STANLEY's TS-620 rifle, which he dangles loosely from one hand.)

GINA: *(To STANLEY)* You're holding it wrong.

STANLEY: All right, all right.

GINA: All these years, you still can't get that right.

STANLEY: It's not a big deal.

GINA: It's not a 520x series pistol! It's a TS-620 rapid repeat blaster rifle!

STANLEY: Can you stop?

GINA: No Corps Fighter in any of the movies ever holds it with one hand, okay? It's too casual, and they're too disciplined. That's all I'm saying.

STANLEY: Great. Thanks. Duly noted.

(GINA nods to the Kookoochik, who is breathing heavily on the couch.)

GINA: Take the mask off this time.

(STANLEY glares at GINA for a moment, and then takes off the Kookoochik's mask. The man underneath gulps a lung-full of fresh air and then starts coughing violently.)

(He is a fashionable, bespectacled man in his fifties. He'd be a very pleasant looking fellow under normal conditions. These, however, are not normal conditions; his glasses are broken and he has a big welt across his cheek. He is SHERMAN.)

SHERMAN: *(Catching his breath)* Jesus!

(SHERMAN is still panting and coughing a bit. STANLEY and GINA do not take off their helmets.)

STANLEY: Just take deep, slow breaths.

GINA: You're fine. Try and relax.

SHERMAN: I'm fine? You two jumped me outside of my car, punched me in the face, shoved me in this costume, pushed me in a trunk, and drove me to God knows where!

STANLEY: We're sorry, Mr Schneider. This wasn't actually our idea.

(The boiler room door opens. BRUCE walks out. His beard is still wild, but he has at least made an effort to clean up and groom himself.)

BRUCE: It was mine.

SHERMAN: Jesus Christ.

BRUCE: Miss me?

SHERMAN: Bruce, I don't believe it! You're dead!

BRUCE: I beg to differ. Geez, you look hot, Sherman. That costume does get warm. I should know. You want something to drink? *(He walks to the mini-fridge.)*

SHERMAN: I went to your memorial service, the funeral...

BRUCE: They usually only let me have water, but maybe I can convince them to let us have something stronger, to mark the occasion.

*(*BRUCE *glances to* STANLEY *and* GINA.*)*

GINA: Maybe just this—

BRUCE: Ah, that's too bad. Water, then. *(He takes two waters out of the mini-fridge and brings them over to the couch, sitting next to* SHERMAN.*)* Drink. You must be dying.

*(*SHERMAN *guzzles the water, wipes his mouth with the back of his hand.)*

SHERMAN: Jesus Christ, Bruce.

BRUCE: You've said that.

SHERMAN: It's been...Jesus, how long now?

BRUCE: Three years. Almost to the day. That's when I was grabbed out of Pasadena Con by our friends here.

SHERMAN: My god. You've been here for three years? *(He looks at* STANLEY *and* GINA.*)* Who are you two? What kind of monsters...what is this? Are you collecting *Space Corps* directors? People will look for me!

BRUCE: Sure they will. For a whole year. And then they'll just stop.

SHERMAN: The case is still open. It's just, the trail went cold.

BRUCE: Yeah, well, it turns out it's not so difficult to keep someone hidden from the authorities so long as you never let them out of your basement and never ask for a ransom.

SHERMAN: I don't believe this. I never gave up hope, Bruce. I didn't. I've never given up hope. Jesus, Bruce, I'm so happy.

BRUCE: Are you? You don't look happy. (*He gets up, takes a leisurely stroll as he talks.*)

SHERMAN: I mean, under the circumstances… but, Bruce, I promise, I'm beyond thrilled to see you.

(BRUCE *waves his hand airily around the room.*)

BRUCE: Note the decor? We are dealing with some hardcore *Space Corps* fans here. Their knowledge of my movies greatly outpaces my own, and I made the shit up. You know, when they first grabbed me, Sherman, I thought you had put them up to it.

SHERMAN: Why would I have you abducted?

BRUCE: I thought it was a prank. You remember our pranks?

SHERMAN: That would be a little extreme for a prank, don't you think?

BRUCE: I don't know. It would be a hell of a good prank. Tie me up, shove me into a basement…steal my franchise.

SHERMAN: Excuse me?

BRUCE: Three years, Sherman. It's only been three years. Hell, I wasn't gone a year, hardly, when you decided that you'd pick up the mantle and write and direct *Space Corps 6* all by yourself.

SHERMAN: I was doing it as a tribute! For you, Bruce! In your memory!

BRUCE: "In my memory," my ass! You forgot me!
Everyone forgot me! I sat down here for three fucking
years, abandoned, while these two assholes kept me
under lock and fucking key! See that door up there,
Sherman? Heavy, heavy oak, inch-thick deadbolt. You
wanna get stuck behind that shit for three years?

SHERMAN: Bruce, we're gonna get you out of here.
We're gonna get you help. (*To* STANLEY *and* GINA)
What did you two do to him?

BRUCE: You know what they did, Sherman? They took
me to the movies. Well, they didn't take me. I turned
some tables on them with the help of their ten year-old
son, and then he and I went to the big opening of *Space
Corps: Chapter 6—A New Beginning.*

SHERMAN: Oh. Um...well, did you like it?

(BRUCE, *smiling maliciously, leans in close to* SHERMAN.)

BRUCE: Tell me, Sherman: is this the face of somebody
who liked it?

SHERMAN: I'm sorry to hear that. I tried to make
the sort of movie I thought you'd make. A natural
continuation of—

BRUCE: Liar! You fucking liar! A continuation? You
even called it *A New Beginning*, you pretentious
shit! I had reams of notes in my office! Outlines and
plot points! You know where they are! A natural
continuation... you dare sit here and hurl that PR
tribute bullshit in MY face, lie to my fucking FACE,
when I know how full of shit you are? You ignored
every page of notes I left behind so you could make
one of your shmaltzy dime-a-dozen feel-good little boy
fantasy films!

SHERMAN: Bruce, movies get rewritten while they're
being shot; did you really think I was going to be

beholden to some stuff a dead guy scribbled onto a legal pad twenty years ago?

BRUCE: I'm not dead!

SHERMAN: How the hell were we supposed to know that? You've been missing for three years! Look, Bruce: we have gone over this, you and I, over this exact thing more times than I can count. *Space Corps* isn't a sacred cow. No movie is! Every film I've ever made has been a different thing by the end of production than it was at the beginning, whether it be in small ways or in a total overhaul.

BRUCE: You can make your movies your way, Sherman, but don't you dare make my movies your way.

SHERMAN: It's not my way! It's THE way! It's how movies are made! It's a collaborative art form, Bruce. Credits take ten minutes to roll on a big-budget action film because there's close to a thousand individual artists who worked on it, probably more. I've said this before, Bruce, but maybe this time you'll hear it: that's why that *Chapter 1 Enhanced Edition* was so offensive to me. You weren't fixing your own mistakes. You were replacing the work of all of the artists who worked on it with you and for you.

STANLEY: Preach!

BRUCE: *(To* STANLEY*)* Shut up, Stanley. *(To* SHERMAN*)* I am a director. I have final say. It is my creative vision. This is the tacit agreement being made by everyone who signs on to work on a film. It is understood that everything that appears and does not appear on screen is subject to the director's whim!

SHERMAN: If you can't have just a little more respect than that for the people propping you up, you should stick to… I don't know… writing and self-publishing novels. That way you'll have done everything on your own with no help from anyone. You are stubborn and arrogant and inflexible, and while I adore that about you personally, it has always held you back professionally. Professional courtesy doesn't just end with how you treat your crew, by the way. You also have a contract with the audience, and that's why everyone dumped on *Space Corps* chapters four and five. It wasn't because your intentions were "misunderstood". It was because you started to misunderstand that contract. Your fans wanted more of the swashbuckling action-adventure pictures the first three *Space Corps* films were, but you decided you were going to start making Shakespearean space tragedies. And buddy: I love you, but you ain't Shakespeare.

GINA: What is that supposed to mean?

SHERMAN: It's a high bar. Nobody expects him to clear it. But dialogue is not his strong suit. Or narrative structure. Or character development. Or complex metaphors. Or… he's not Shakespeare, that's all I'm saying. And nobody wanted him to be.

(SHERMAN *turns back to* BRUCE.)

SHERMAN: *Space Corps* is supposed to take place in a universe where good is good and bad is bad and everyone knows which is which. Your audience didn't want a *Space Corps* dressed up in the same shades of grey they see every night on the news! (*He stands up and speaks directly into* BRUCE's *face. Firmly*) I brought the franchise back to where it belongs. If you want to call that "little boy fantasy shit," go ahead. I call it a crowd pleasing popcorn picture, and I stand by it, and I'm sorry, but…I'm not sorry.

BRUCE: Crowd-pleasing popcorn garbage would not have inspired the loyalty and passion I've seen out of these two over the past three years. The correct ending to the *Space Corps* saga—

SHERMAN: Jesus, Bruce, it's a movie, there's no "correct" way to—

BRUCE: The CORRECT ending, outlined in the notes you ignored, would have seen Princess Mia Solaria rise up to the rank of Solar Monarch, becoming the corrupt force of evil that she and Link Cloudbringer had always sworn to destroy! The Paladin and the Monarch, locked in combat! Two lovers in a tragic duel for the fate of the galaxy! You, you son of a bitch, gave them a HAPPY ending! In YOUR version, a cackling new villain appeared from out of nowhere, and the Queen, the Paladin, and that bargain basement Yano Deuce replacement you came up with all teamed up to beat the bad guy and save the day in one hundred and eight safe, predictable minutes! Piddling fucking trite-ass bullshit! And you know the worst part of it, Sherman? Do you? *(He grabs* SHERMAN *by the collar and shakes him.)* I ALREADY MADE THAT FUCKING MOVIE, YOU THIEVING PIECE OF ABSOLUTE HORSESHIT!

*(*BRUCE *shoves* SHERMAN *back down onto the couch, hard.* SHERMAN *is speechless with fright.* BRUCE *steps back, taking a moment to settle himself.)*

BRUCE: *(Calmly) Space Corps Chapter 1: The Pirate's Apprentice* was beat-for-beat the same film as *A New Beginning,* and you know it. You KNOW it. You're not COMPLETELY stupid. You passed at least ONE course at UCLA, right? You passed Screen Composition for Pretentious Mouth-Breathers, didn't you? That was a 100-level course, wasn't it? Screen Composition for Pretentious Mouth-Breathers? You passed that one, right, Sherman?

STANLEY: *(Aside to* GINA*)* Is that really a course?

GINA: Shut up, Stanley.

SHERMAN: It's what the studio wanted. The fans were ready to revolt. They were ready to—

BRUCE: —kidnap me to keep me from ever making another *Space Corps* movie again.

(SHERMAN *turns to* STANLEY *and* GINA.)

SHERMAN: Is that what this is all about?

BRUCE: It is. Joke's on them, though. You pinched out a log not even I would have stunk up the theater with.

SHERMAN: So you didn't like it. Fine. The fans love it. Did you see the early reviews? "A return to *Space Corps* form." That's from the Times. "The *Space Corps* we know and love, back again." That's from the Post.

BRUCE: Those are critic's reviews, Sherman. I think someone hasn't looked at the aggregated "Fan-o-Meter" score, which is hovering, last we checked, around thirty-eight percent positive.

SHERMAN: That's it? They didn't like it? (*He looks to* GINA *and* STANLEY.) You didn't like it?

(GINA *and* STANLEY *look at each other and take off their helmets.*)

STANLEY: It was redundant.

GINA: You really thought what the fans wanted was MORE CGI?

STANLEY: And a NEW Pirate's Apprentice? What's the point?

GINA: I liked that this one was a woman.

STANLEY: Sure, fine. But where was Yano Deuce?

GINA: He barely even had a cameo! We named our son after him, and you made him inconsequential.

SHERMAN: You named your son Yano?

STANLEY: It's a normal name!

GINA: The worst, though, is what you did to poor Ding Dong Diggum. Decapitating him like that in the first five minutes of the movie. Children love him.

STANLEY: You done did Ding Dong Diggum dirty, dude.

SHERMAN: The fans hate Ding Dong! That was my slam dunk! That was the thing everyone was going to love!

STANLEY: We didn't.

GINA: We thought we would, but we didn't.

BRUCE: Let this be a lesson, Sherman. You can please some of the fans all of the time, you can please all of the fans some of the time, but you can always piss off all of the fans at the same time, even if you're giving them exactly what they're begging for. They thought they wanted you to take over *Space Corps*, Sherman. I knew better, though, didn't I? For years you begged me to let you direct a chapter, but I knew what sort of fetid upchuck you'd hork out of your face-hole. I knew all you had in you was a cheap copy of what I'd already done, layered over with your signature blend of obvious nostalgia and pandering earnestness. You gave a goddamn World War 2 movie a happy ending, Sherman. Fucking Nazis, and you found the silver lining.

(SHERMAN *is too terrified to speak.* BRUCE *lazily crosses behind him.)*

BRUCE: I know what you're thinking. You're thinking, "Is this for real? Or is Bruce playing the long-game for the king of all pranks?"

SHERMAN: Wait…no…is this…?

BRUCE: No, Sherman, this isn't the prank. You know what the prank is?

(BRUCE *pulls the sharpened replica Black Hole assassin's knife from behind his back, grabs* SHERMAN *by the scalp, and in one quick motion, he slices* SHERMAN's *throat.* SHERMAN *falls to the floor, gurgling and gasping, blood squirting everywhere.*)

GINA: What the fuck?!

STANLEY: Oh God, I'm gonna be sick.

(STANLEY *throws up behind the couch.* BRUCE *comes around the couch, and crouches down next to his old friend's dying form, looking at it pitifully.*)

BRUCE: The prank, Sherman, was you fooling a major film studio into thinking you have in your entire body even one iota of the amount of talent I have in my left testicle.

(BRUCE *reaches out and cradles* SHERMAN's *terrified face with one hand.*)

BRUCE: You don't deserve *Space Corps*, Sherman. You never did.

(SHERMAN *gives one last pathetic gurgle, a final shuddering heave, and then lays still, his body growing cold in a pool of his own blood.*)

(BRUCE *stands. He wipes some blood brusquely off on his pants.*)

BRUCE: He got blood on me. Son of a bitch can't even die without being an asshole about it. (*He looks at* STANLEY *and* GINA.) Where'd you dump the car?

STANLEY: ...Wh...what?

GINA: It's still in the garage.

BRUCE: Not this time. Last time. After you kidnapped me. Where'd you dump it? Forget it, it doesn't matter. Just dump this one somewhere else. And get this useless sack of meat into the trunk before you do. I'll replace the carpeting and the couch. We can burn these

in the woods or something. I have money tucked away.
God bless the Swiss. What's wrong with you two?

(GINA *is sitting on the back of the couch, in shock.* STANLEY
is on his knees, crying silently to himself.)

STANLEY: What's wrong with us?! You just fucking slit
your friend's fucking throat!

BRUCE: And you've kept me prisoner in your basement
for three years. You turn me in for killing this meatbag,
and your kid grows up visiting his parents once a
month at the state penitentiary for the next thirty plus
years. Comprende?

(GINA *and* STANLEY *nod.*)

BRUCE: Good. Get to work. And know this: we are a
team now. We are bound by this. And as long as we
are stuck in this together, let's be productive about it.
Let's make sure that nobody, and I mean nobody, ever
makes another *Space Corps* movie again unless it's the
one we decide they will make. I'm hungry. You guys
got any cold cuts? (*He climbs the stairs to the door, opens
it up, and heads into the house.*)

STANLEY: Oh my God.

GINA: I know. We're gonna make a *Space Corps* movie
with Bruce Glover!

(*An excited* GINA *runs up and out the door after* BRUCE.
STANLEY *throws up again.* SHERMAN's *body lies on the
ground, beginning to decompose on a microscopic level.*)

(*Blackout*)

Interlude #6

(Follow spot up on a professional-looking woman in her late forties/early fifties standing DS. She wears a headset microphone and is dressed smartly business casual.)

(She is KYLA KERNEY, *the new CEO of GloverFilm.)*

KYLA: Hello. I'm Kyla Kerney.

(Polite applause. KYLA *waits for it to die down.)*

KYLA: Today is a very exciting day. For the past four years I've served as CEO of GloverFilm, a division of Wally Boys Entertainment. Usually when I come onstage at the WallyWorld Expo, it's to tell you about a new video game, or a television project, or a comic book. Tonight is different. Our last visit to the stars was, to quote the great Bruce Glover, "Many years ago, and in a universe beyond our own." Five years, to be precise. The late Sherman Schneider's final film, *Space Corps Chapter 6: The New Beginning* was a box office blockbuster and a rollicking adventure that reminds us all why we love *Space Corps* as much as we do. Sadly, the *Space Corps* franchise has been darkened by too many off-screen clouds over the past several years: the disappearance of Bruce Glover, and the tragic death of Sherman Schneider. Indeed, the Internet likes to tell us that the *Space Corps* franchise is cursed. Well. I'm still here, aren't I?

(Polite applause)

KYLA: Thank you. Yes, I'm still here, and I'm here with a very important message: not only is the *Space Corps* franchise not cursed, but it is very much alive! I am proud to announce today that we here at Wally Boys have recently entered pre-production on the highly anticipated *Space Corps Chapter 7*!

(A fanfare of music, the Space Corps theme, flourishes to life as the audience audibly gasps, followed by a round of

raucous cheering and applause. KYLA *soaks it in. Finally, it dies down. The Space Corps theme song lowers in volume, continuing to play under* KYLA*'s continued spiel.)*

KYLA: I am as excited as you are. We have just begun pre-production on the as-of-yet untitled *Space Corps Chapter 7,* and I don't have many details to share aside from a promise that you can get ready for launch in two years from this exact date: May third. We have a script and some high profile directors all competing to take the reins. We couldn't be more excited here at GloverFilm, and none of this would be happening if it wasn't for you: the fans.

(Wild applause)

KYLA: Yes, yes. Give yourselves a hand. You've earned it.

(The applause dies down.)

KYLA: You'll be hearing more from me very soon. Until then…

(A stage crew member runs out to KYLA *holding a prop Sun Sword. She takes it and holds it up awkwardly in an en-garde position.)*

KYLA: "Will the light shine your way home."

(Wild applause)

(Blackout)

Scene 2

(The basement. It has been five years since SHERMAN*'s untimely demise. In the basement are* BRUCE, *well-groomed and looking good, and* YANO, *now fifteen years old. The basement has been given a makeover, and has been spiffed up over the last five years.)*

(BRUCE and YANO are playing a video game on BRUCE's TV. Explosions, sound FX, and triumphant music all pour out from the TV in beautiful digital sound.)

BRUCE: Oh, you are dead. I've got you now.

YANO: I don't think so, old man.

(The SFX of a spaceship screaming past overhead emanates from the game, followed by a string of explosion SFXs.)

BRUCE: Wait, what'd you just do?!

YANO: I called in Kaszuba to do a flyby in the Century Crow. Your ass just got napalmed back to Banoo.

BRUCE: *(Laughing)* Son of a…I am never going to get the hang of these things.

YANO: You're getting better.

BRUCE: Don't patronize me. My generation will never be good at video games. We passed them by in our rush to adulthood. I should have played more *Pong* at my college-years dive bar.

YANO: What's *Pong*?

BRUCE: Ping-pong, minus the fun. Want to go again?

YANO: Sure.

(BRUCE and YANO start up a new round. SFX burst back into life.)

BRUCE: I can't get over how incredible these games look. *Space Corps* video games have come a long way since the days of black-and-white stick figures waving around smaller sticks. Oh, shit, are you really playing as Ding-Dong Diggum?

YANO: I thought I'd make it a fair fight.

BRUCE: Teenagers. You guys sure are assholes.

YANO: *(Grinning)* We sure are.

(BRUCE *and* YANO *play for a few moments, focused in on the action.)*

BRUCE: Did you ever go back and argue that grade with your media studies teacher?

YANO: He won't budge. He says my thesis is fundamentally flawed. He insists that *Citizen Kane* came too early in Orson Welles' career to be considered his greatest work. Says there's no way Welles had matured enough as an artist by that point.

BRUCE: What does he think Welles' greatest work is?

YANO: *Touch of Evil.*

BRUCE: Which is a fine film but, goddamn it, man. *Kane* invented modern cinema. No director would be telling stories as we are today without *Citizen Kane*. Forced perspective, deep focus, age make-up, flashbacks, flash-forwards, extreme angles… the list is nearly endless.

YANO: He also said that *Citizen Kane* is way too popular to be Welles' greatest film.

(BRUCE *throws his controller down in mock anger that is also a little bit real.)*

YANO: You're going to lose!

BRUCE: I was going to lose anyway. He actually said that to you?

YANO: He did.

BRUCE: That is such bullshit it's not even funny. Just because something is POPULAR doesn't mean it can't also be GOOD.

YANO: He said after that he was only kidding, but I don't think he was.

BRUCE: Good God, how do I get a high school media studies teacher fired?

YANO: *(Giggling)* You could slit his throat.

BRUCE: *(Smirking)* Don't you let your mother hear you talking like that. What the fuck is "media studies," anyway? *(He picks his controller back up.)* Let's go again, and this time I'll go easy on you.

YANO: You will try.

(The basement door swings open. GINA bursts in.)

GINA: It's happening!

BRUCE: What is?

GINA: Guess.

BRUCE: They've done it? They announced it?

GINA: Kyla Kerner just got on stage at the WallyWorld Expo and announced that *Space Corps: Chapter 7* is in pre-production!

BRUCE: This is it! This is where it starts!

YANO: Up top, Bruce! Let's go!

(BRUCE and YANO high five.)

BRUCE: Have they named a date yet?

GINA: Two years from today.

BRUCE: May third. They must have a director in place already, no?

GINA: None that they've announced.

BRUCE: Could it really be this easy?

GINA: I hope so.

BRUCE: C'mere, you.

(BRUCE sweeps GINA into an old-school dip, and they kiss, deep and passionately.)

YANO: Ugh. Get a room!

(BRUCE and GINA come up laughing.)

BRUCE: Maybe later, we will.

YANO: Gross!

GINA: Two years, though.

BRUCE: I thought it would be three. We have to move fast.

GINA: Can we even wait for them to name a director? She says there's a lot of A-listers jockeying for the spot.

BRUCE: Either she's bluffing, or they've hired somebody and they're trying to keep it quiet for as long as they can, trying to hide the scent, confuse whoever it is that keeps making their directors disappear. You know: you. And whats-his-name... Stanley. May he rest in peace.

(YANO *guffaws.*)

GINA: You are so wicked.

BRUCE: I thought you liked me wicked.

(GINA *sidles up to* BRUCE.)

GINA: Mmmm...maybe I do.

(BRUCE *and* GINA *are about to kiss again, when...*)

STANLEY: *(OS)* Honey? You down there?

(BRUCE *and* GINA *jump apart.* STANLEY *appears at the top of the steps.*)

STANLEY: Hey, what's going on down here?

GINA: *(Flustered)* Nothing, just some stuff, normal stuff, why?

BRUCE: *(Not flustered)* Kyla Kerney just went onstage at the WallyWorld Expo and announced a new *Space Corps* movie.

STANLEY: *(Taken aback)* Oh.

YANO: Pretty great, right?

STANLEY: Yeah, sure. Great.

BRUCE: We should start planning immediately.

STANLEY: Yes.

BRUCE: Who's hungry? Pizza tonight?

YANO: No, Chinese.

BRUCE: Them's fighting words, boy.

YANO: Bring it, old man!

(BRUCE *and* YANO *playfight.* STANLEY *looks on, Eeyore-like.*)

GINA: The both of you, stop. When you two get started, I swear. Come on, we'll go upstairs and look at menus.

BRUCE: I'm right with you, Gina.

(*Chattering happily,* GINA, BRUCE, *and* YANO *head up the stairs, leaving a lonely* STANLEY *behind.*)

STANLEY: (*Calling after them*) Maybe we should just let it be.

(*Nobody responds.*)

STANLEY: How about barbecue?

(*Nobody responds.*)

(*Blackout*)

Interlude #7

(*In the blackout:*)

KYLA: (*VO*) "Hi, you've reached Kyla Kerney. Please leave a message, and will the light shine your way home."

(KYLA *walks on, looking down at her smartphone as her voicemails play. She stops DSR and listens.*)

(*SFX: A voicemail BEEEP!*)

VOICEMAIL #1: *(VO)* Kyla, hey, it's James. Look, I appreciate you thinking of me, and I can see how a sci-fi fantasy space opera could be a good fit, but I'm really more into exploring the ocean in my little submarine these days and tricking movie studios into paying for it. Put a shipwreck into *Space Corps* somehow and maybe we can talk. Look: I love the franchise, I grew up on it, but… you know, those fans are never happy with anything, and also I don't want to vanish mysteriously. Okay, call me.

(KYLA taps the screen.)

(SFX: A voicemail BEEEP!)

VOICEMAIL #2: *(VO)* Ms Kerney, this is Guillermo. I have considered your offer and I am afraid I must decline. I have very great respect for *Space Corps* and the legacy of Bruce Glover, but after careful consideration I just can't see how my personal aesthetic fits the *Space Corps* universe. *Space Corps* is about the personal struggles of heroes and legends as they clash on the grandest battlefield. I'd mostly be interested in what those heroes dream about, how many puppets I could use to portray those dreams, and which character is most likely to fall in love with a fish. Also, I do not wish to vanish mysteriously. Muchas gracias.

(KYLA taps the screen again.)

(SFX: A voicemail BEEEP!)

VOICEMAIL #3 *(VO)* 'Sup, babe, it's Michael. Look, it's a no-go for me on that space stuff. I'm more of a giant robot kind of guy, and let's keep it one-hundred: *Space Corps* is too family-friendly for me. I'd need to throw in way more titties and explosions than you guys would be comfortable with… (I sure do love me some fuckin' titties) …and Wally Boys ain't gonna go for it. Buncha' fuckin' Mormons over there. Also…and it would be impossible for me to overemphasize this, but on the

really-real real? I do NOT wanna vanish mysteriously.
Deuces out, homey-slice.

(KYLA taps the screen again. This time, her phone speaks.)

AUTOMATED OPERATOR: *(VO)* End of messages.

KYLA: God damn it. Where the hell is he?

(Blackout)

Scene 3

*(Lights up on the basement. The usual procession has
already reached the bottom of the steps: two head-to-
toe armored Corps Fighters, one holding the leash of a
Kookoochik, and one holding a prop replica blaster rifle...
only, oddly enough, the armed Corps Fighter is actually
holding his rifle properly, with two hands.)*

(The Kookoochik points at the couch.)

KYLA: *(In the Kookoochik costume)* Here?

GINA: Sure, that's fine.

*(The Kookoochik [KYLA] moves around and stands in front
of the couch, taking off the mask as she does, but she does not
sit down. The two Corps Fighters also remove their helmets;
underneath are GINA...and YANO.)*

KYLA: I wouldn't be here, but I'm desperate. *(She looks
around, taking in her surroundings. She makes a face.)* I
don't know if I'm THIS desperate, though.

(BRUCE steps out of the boiler room.)

BRUCE: Are you sure?

(KYLA shrugs.)

KYLA: *(Non-plussed)* No. That, again, is why I'm here.

(BRUCE is puzzled by KYLA's lack of reaction.)

BRUCE: *(To GINA)* Did you tell her about me?

GINA: We just grabbed her and dragged her to the car. She put the suit on herself.

KYLA: Yeah, and it's hot as a donkey's nutsack in here. Kid, get over here, help me get this thing off.

(YANO *hurries over and helps* KYLA *out of the suit.*)

KYLA: Great, thanks, that's great. *(She turns to* BRUCE.*)* So. What's up?

BRUCE: "What's up?" That's it? I'm back from the dead and all you've got to say is, "What's up?"

KYLA: Back from the dead? They never found a body. I figured you either got sick of the whole thing and ran off with your millions of dollars, or some crazy fan kidnapped you so you could make movies just for them.

GINA: You're at least one-third right.

KYLA: So when a couple of cosplayers tried to grab me outside my condo, emphasis on "tried"…

YANO: She tased me.

KYLA: *(To* YANO*)* You had it coming. *(To* BRUCE*)* Once I had my wits about me, I realized what was happening. I had been expecting to hear from you, Bruce. I was wondering how you'd make contact. "Grabbed by cultists" was, like, third on my list.

YANO: What was first and second?

KYLA: Snail mail, but with all the letters cut out from a magazine like a serial killer, or Western Union.

BRUCE: You're bullshitting us.

KYLA: Oh, no. I know better than to bullshit a bullshitter. Schneider was your doing, wasn't it? They pulled him out of a lake with his head half cut off. You hated his movie, was that it?

BRUCE: I don't know what you're talking about.

KYLA: Sure you don't. *(She looks around.)* Cozy place you've got here. And by cozy, I mean deeply disturbing. *(To* GINA*)* Is this about the sex for you, or is it more of a hero worship thing?

GINA: What? No! It's not…it's… *(She sighs.)* …it's a little of both.

KYLA: *(To* YANO*)* And what's your deal?

YANO: My parents named me Yano. Middle name Deuce.

KYLA: Ooo, that would fuck me up, too.

*(*STANLEY *enters at the top of the steps. He wears a Corps Fighter helmet but no armor; he is dressed otherwise in his normal clothes.* KYLA *sees him.)*

KYLA: You guys making a low budget fan film? Could only afford two whole sets of armor?

GINA: Stanley, what are you doing?

STANLEY: Do NOT use my real name!

GINA: We all have our masks off.

STANLEY: Why would you do that?!

GINA: Just get down here; you're so embarrassing!

*(*STANLEY *hurries down the steps as* KYLA *turns to* BRUCE*.)*

KYLA: *(To* BRUCE*)* Let's get to it. Are you gonna come direct my movie?

BRUCE: YOUR movie? *Space Corps* is my—

KYLA: Cut it with the artist's ownership crap, okay? I've got the intellectual property rights and I'm not the one who's been hanging out on the back of a milk carton for seven years.

BRUCE: Coming back is not quite the idea we had in mind. I feel as though re-emerging might get… complicated.

KYLA: Oh, so what is "the idea"? Why am I here?

BRUCE: We, the four of us together, want to act as unofficial consultants to the new film. We saw Sherman's quaint attempt at a *Space Corps* movie, God rest his soul. While I don't want to speak ill of the dead...

KYLA: ...even though you're about to.

(BRUCE *clears his throat.*)

BRUCE: Well, nevertheless, thereabouts being neither here nor there...we all—

GINA: *(Interjecting)* All four of us!

BRUCE: Of course, the four of us. While I don't know what you're implying in regards to Sherman's untimely demise, certainly we had nothing to do with that... we all did feel that Sherman wasn't quite able in his effort to capture the true essence of *Space Corps*. That *je ne sais quoi* that makes *Space Corps* great.

KYLA: Neither did you, those last two times out.

BRUCE: Now, hold on...

YANO: *Chapters 4* and *5* are the best!

GINA: Well...

(GINA *glances at* BRUCE *uncomfortably as he visibly scowls. This is still a point of contention between them.*)

KYLA: Whatever, okay? I don't care. I actually don't give a single little shit. You can all have your own personal "*Space Corps* Ranking" list, which is the best one, which is the worst one, which one you got to first base during, but if I'm being completely honest? I've never managed to sit all the way through an entire *Space Corps* movie. Bores the crap out of me.

GINA: *(Horrified)* How can you run a franchise you don't even like?!

KYLA: Franchises exist...do you have something to drink? I'm parched.

BRUCE: Stan.

(STANLEY hurries over to the mini-fridge, gets a bottle of water for KYLA.)

KYLA: Thanks, dummy. Anyway. Franchises exist to make money. I have time and again proven to my bosses that I know how to do that. With a property like *Space Corps*, it's almost too easy. I could dig up a Malaysian snuff film from somewhere, not that I have a bunch in my attic or anything, but I could dig one up, roll it out under the name *Space Corps*, and I'd STILL break a billion dollars worldwide in my goddamn sleep. In my SLEEP, Bruce.

GINA: Not if the product isn't any good, you wouldn't! Fans would boycott!

KYLA: It is adorable that you think that. *Space Corps* isn't a movie series anymore to people like you. It is a religion, and each movie that comes out is an act of God that must be sanctified. These fans are addicts and as much as they're trying to kick the habit? They need their hit, man, and they gonna answer that door when the snowman comes a'knockin'. You know all of the grown-ass man-children screaming on social media that they'll never pay to see another *Space Corps* movie again because the last one, "raped their childhood?" We have those guys for life, no matter how much they swear they hate us. It's the CASUAL fans we need to worry about. What the die-hards want doesn't mean shit, because let's face it: they don't know what they want. No, that's wrong. They know EXACTLY what they want. They each want the individual private *Space Corps* movie that they've all of them already written and directed in their minds. Even if I could read minds I'd only be able to make one fan happy at a time, so why the hell should I kill myself trying to satisfy their endless demands?

GINA: This is outrageous. The disrespect you have for your most loyal fans is… I actually feel nauseous.

KYLA: Perhaps, and yet? Do stop me whence I tell a lie. Of course, the real money isn't at the theater, it's in the merchandising. You primed the pump but good for us, Bruce. You conditioned an entire generation of fans to buy up any old crap you could brand with the words *"Space Corps"*, and now all of that earning potential sits under the singular Wally Boys umbrella, from beneath which we will sell, amongst other things, *Space Corps* umbrellas. Infinite possibilities yielding infinite profit. Bruce, I desperately want to turn your franchise into the never-ending milk-giving goat's teet I know it can be, but first I need to jump start this new wave of product with the crown jewel of the collection: a brand new *Space Corps* film. Unfortunately, and through no fault of my own? I can not find a single A-list director willing to take the job. None of them want to vanish mysteriously.

STANLEY: Don't worry. Our kidnapping days are over.

KYLA: Really? They are? As of today? Remind me again how I got here.

GINA: That's not our fault. Things keep coming up.

BRUCE: Your new director would not vanish.

KYLA: I don't think they're gonna take your word for it. If I bring in some amateur nobody to helm this film, and those guys are dime-a-dozen, the Internets will freaking explode.

GINA: I thought you didn't care what we fans think. I thought you had us "for life."

KYLA: What's your Flitter name?

GINA: Why does that matter?

KYLA: Come on, what is it?

GINA: ...At-Mia-Solaria-Girl-Power-X-O.

KYLA: I have you for life. I have everyone for life who has a social media name that plays on a reference to anything from *Space Corps*. But you know studios, Bruce. Wally Boys doesn't have the stomach for riling up the web nerds with our first big production decision. Snagging a top director to excite the fanbase is literally my only mandate from on high and now? Here you are. Bruce Glover, back from exile, out of the desert, manna from heaven.

BRUCE: Kyla, I just can't. It would be too complicated.

KYLA: Complicated. Maybe you're right. Maybe the circumstances of your disappearance were so mysterious that it would be just too darn "complicated" for you to come back. Or let's consider something else for a hot second. Maybe, Bruce, you're not gonna come back because you're addicted to twenty-four seven access to crazy fan pussy.

STANLEY: What is that supposed to mean?

KYLA: *(To* STANLEY*)* Open your eyes, cuck. *(To* BRUCE*)* I don't care to understand why you want to stay in this fucking basement. I draw my salary every day whether *Space Corps 7* makes it to theaters or not. But it's going to make my life one-thousand times easier if I can walk you into Wally Boys, the prodigal son returned by my hand. You'll get a hero's welcome, Bruce. I'll even have studio PR and legal deflect whatever questions anyone might have to ask about your dear departed friend Sherman.

STANLEY: We have not kept this man locked in our house for all of these years just so he could go back and do exactly what we wanted to keep him from doing!

KYLA: What's that?

BRUCE: Make another *Space Corps*. They really didn't like 4 and 5.

GINA: Stanley, this time we'll be involved, too! We can make sure it goes right! It'll be the *Space Corps* movie we always dreamed of, because we'll be secret consultants, along with Bruce!

KYLA: Yeah, let's talk about this "secret consultant" bullshit. I have zero interest in that. Have I not made that clear? Allow me to do so: I have zero interest, Bruce, in bringing on you and your harem as "secret consultants." I want you to come back to civilization and direct the next chapter of *Space Corps*. That's it. That's the deal. Direct the movie, or go fuck yourself. What do you say?

BRUCE: I just… don't see how it's possible.

KYLA: So go fuck yourself.

(GINA *takes* BRUCE *by the hand.*)

GINA: It could be wonderful, though. It could be the best of both worlds. We'd just have to come up with the right cover story.

STANLEY: Gina, are you insane? We kidnapped the man and have held him hostage for eight years! We are accessories to murder! And we have seriously, seriously messed up our kid! If we let him leave, we will be found out. There is no cover story we can concoct that will explain away the last eight years! We would go to jail, Gina. Do you understand that? If Bruce Glover is allowed to return to the world, you and I will go to jail!

GINA: Maybe—

STANLEY: No maybes! He isn't leaving. (*He turns to* KYLA.)I shouldn't even let you leave.

KYLA: Try and stop me, sweetie.

(STANLEY *and* KYLA *step towards each other.* BRUCE *gets in between them.*)

BRUCE: No! Stanley, Kyla! No!

(BRUCE *pulls* STANLEY *away.*)

BRUCE: Stanley, you're right. *(He turns to* KYLA.*)* He's right. I can't. I can't re-emerge without an explanation, and we don't have one, not one that would stand up to scrutiny. It would tear this family apart.

KYLA: Wow.

BRUCE: I know it seems crazy, but…

(BRUCE *looks to* GINA *and* YANO.*)

BRUCE: …I can't do that. Not to them.

KYLA: Stockholm Syndrome much, Bruce? Fine. Whatever. Now I think of it, I'm sure I can get some slasher film hack-of-the-moment to sign on as director. I could probably sell the studio on hiring a hot-hand young-gun B-movie guy.

BRUCE: You wouldn't!

KYLA: Surely I would. We'll spin it as, "*Space Corps* crosses genres. Horror meets sci-fi/fantasy. A mature new direction for the legacy franchise." *(She imagines this and nods.)* Yeah. I can sell that. Unless, of course… you have another directorial suggestion? Perhaps the man who created this franchise in the first place? And none of this "secret consultant" crap. Either you're my face-out director or you're just another fanboy in his basement. There's no in-between.

(BRUCE *seethes, but has no response.*)

KYLA: You didn't think this through, Bruce. You wanted to have your cake and eat it, too. But if you couldn't stand *Space Corps* as made by Sherman

Schneider, what made you think you'd be able to sit in some weird-ass secret co-pilot's seat for anybody else? You can either keep your twisted little Manson family and sit on the sidelines watching as I make whatever goddamn *Space Corps* movie I want… or you can stop being a ridiculous little bitch, man-up, and get back in the game. Your choice.

(Nobody likes this, but nobody has anything left to say. KYLA *looks back and forth at them all and shrugs.)*

KYLA: Okay. Done. I'm out. *(She starts climbing the steps.)*I'll walk a few blocks away before calling my car. Don't worry; I won't blow up your spot. If you're not coming back it would hardly be worth the trouble of revealing you're still alive. Can you even imagine all the press I'd have to deal with? Fuck that noise right in the ass. *(She stops at the top of the steps and looks down at the rest of them.)* I'll wait a week. One week, Bruce, for you to change your mind. Think about it. Also? This basement stinks. Badly. Smells. Do something about that. You're still human beings, for God's sake.

GINA: What if you're wrong?

KYLA: Okay, you're not human beings. Whatever, babe.

GINA: What if you're wrong about *Space Corps*? What if you and your attitude and all you care about is money, what if that all leads to a bunch of movies that are so awful that the fans stop caring and then stop coming? What happens then? What will you do? What will WE do?

KYLA: I will get a golden parachute and a six picture deal with another studio. You? You'll fall into a depression and kill yourself. I dunno. Jesus. They're just movies.

(KYLA exits. Silence in the basement.)

STANLEY: She's kinda right, isn't she?

GINA: About what?

STANLEY: About everything.

(BRUCE *and* GINA *look incredulously at* STANLEY.)

STANLEY: What? She didn't bite, guys. We're not working on *Space Corps*. That's it. It's over. We may as well get comfortable, because now we're all trapped here together. Forever.

(STANLEY *begins to climb the steps.* GINA *reaches for him.*)

GINA: Stanley, sweetie—

(STANLEY *jerks away.*)

STANLEY: "Sweetie"? Are you kidding me? (*He sighs.*) Do you know what I miss? I miss being able to sit down and watch a *Space Corps* movie without worrying what everyone else thinks of it. I miss being able to watch a *Space Corps* movie without worrying what I think of it. I'm exhausted. (*He leaves.*)

(*Blackout*)

Interlude #8

(*Spot up DS. A podcast studio. Smoke fills the air.* JEB DUTT *is podcasting, alongside his co-host* PATTY AMADA *and* SEBASTIAN WATTS. *All three sit in front of mounted microphones, wearing headsets.*)

JEB DUTT: This is Jeb Dutt alongside my BFFs Patty Amada...

PATTY AMADA: Hey hey.

JEB DUTT: ...and Sebastian Watts.

SEBASTIAN WATTS: "Watts" up, everybody?

JEB DUTT: ...and you're listening to *The Corps Report*, the Internet's twelfth most popular *Space Corps* podcast. Now, okay, it has been super quiet out of

GloverFilm since *SpaceCorps 7* was announced by Kyla Kerney at WallyWorld. Since then, like, not a peep. What is up with that, man?

PATTY AMADA: I know, it's ridiculous. Why isn't she letting us know what's going on with *Chapter 7* every hour on the hour? What does she have to do, spend time with her family?

SEBASTIAN WATTS: I'm telling you, Wally Boys has gotta remove Kyla Kerney from GloverFilm. She has no idea what she's doing. Like, there's all this buzz going around about how she can't find a director. How hard can it be to find someone to direct a *Space Corps* movie? Directors have to be lining up and banging down her door and she can't find someone?

PATTY AMADA: What do you think of that list of rumored directors that got leaked onto Reddit?

JEB DUTT: They all suck. Every last one of them. If she hires any of those guys I'm gonna boycott *Chapter 7*, no doubt.

SEBASTIAN WATTS: Same, dude. Same.

JEB DUTT: Kyla Kerney is just so full of shit. She's not going to revive *Space Corps*.

PATTY AMADA: Yep.

JEB DUTT: She doesn't even like *Space Corps*.

PATTY AMADA: She does not.

JEB DUTT: She just knows she has to PRETEND to care about *Space Corps* so she doesn't LOSE the fans, because that's what ALL of this is about: US. The FANS. And what WE WANT.

SEBASTIAN WATTS: Amen, brother!

PATTY AMADA: Preach! Testify!

JEB DUTT: Yeah! Oh, uh… *(Reading copy)* It's also about our sponsor today. Patty?

PATTY AMADA: *(Also reading copy)* That's right, Jeb. Today's sponsor of the pod is Needy Boy Adult Diapers. Needy Boy: When you gotta go, and everyone has to know…strap on a pair of Needy Boys!

(Blackout)

(In the darkness…)

KYLA: *(VO)* Hi, you've reached Kyla Kerney. Please leave a message, and will the light shine your way home.

(The voicemail beeps.)

BRUCE: *(VO)* Kyla, it's Bruce. I'll see you soon.

(A click, as BRUCE hangs up.)

Scene 4

(The basement. It is empty and the lights are off, but the display case lights are on. One of the displays is open. From off-stage:)

STANLEY: *(OS)* Hey, I'm back! I've got dinner!

(Beat. No response)

STANLEY: *(OS)* Hello? Guys? Dinner!

(Beat. No response)

STANLEY: *(OS)* Where is everybody?

(Beat. No response)

(The door at the top of the stairs opens up. STANLEY is framed in the light from upstairs.)

STANLEY: Are you down here?

(No response. STANLEY is about to turn but then notices the display case.)

STANLEY: Are you kidding? *(Calling out)* Yano, what have I told you a million times? Mommy and daddy's toys aren't toys! *(He heads down the steps and crosses to the display case.)* For Pete's— *(He crosses back to the stairs and yells up.)* Yano, where is the TS-620 blaster rifle replica? Bring it back down here right now!

(Suspenseful music from Space Corps: Chapter 3 begins to play in the dark.)

STANLEY: What the... ?

(The boiler room door opens and STANLEY jumps. BRUCE, GINA, and YANO emerge from the boiler room. They are each in full Space Corps cosplay. GINA as Mia Solaria, BRUCE as Yano Deuce [complete with poncho], and YANO as Ding-Dong Diggum. BRUCE steps forward to STANLEY. YANO positions himself as BRUCE's eager sidekick. GINA hangs back, watching silently, inscrutable.)

STANLEY: Cripes, you guys scared me. What are you doing down here in the dark? Why are you in costume?

BRUCE: First of all, Stanley, I want you to know that this is not personal.

STANLEY: What? I got barbecue. Come upstairs. Yano, are you really dressed as Ding-Dong Diggum?

YANO: So?

STANLEY: I can't even with you. Where's the TS-620?

BRUCE: He doesn't have it. I do. *(He pulls the TS-620 replica rifle out from under his poncho.)*

STANLEY: But you're dressed as Yano Deuce. The TS-620 is a Corps Fighter weapon.

(STANLEY reaches over and takes the TS-620 from BRUCE.)

STANLEY: Yano Deuce doesn't use one of these. And that poncho is the wrong color. This cosplay is straight-up trash, Bruce.

BRUCE: You know, Stanley, when you're right, you're right. I guess you're just a bigger fan than I am.

STANLEY: Yeah. Now stop skulking around down here, all of you. It's dinner time.

BRUCE: We're not going upstairs, Stanley. Not yet.

STANLEY: What, you want to eat down here? Just like the good old days, huh, Bruce? You wanna lock yourself in your basement again? Fine with me.

BRUCE: We're not going upstairs because the police are going to be here any minute now.

STANLEY: Excuse me?

BRUCE: You were right, Stan. I can't return to the world without at least one of us turning ourselves in.

STANLEY: One of us?

BRUCE: So we called the police. Told them what's been going on here these past eight years. Told them where to find us.

STANLEY: Oh my God.

BRUCE: I'm sorry it's come to this, Stanley.

YANO: I'm not.

STANLEY: Don't talk to me while you're dressed like that.

BRUCE: I'd thank you not to use that tone with my son, Stanley.

STANLEY: Your son? What the hell does that mean?

BRUCE: You have a choice now. You and Gina can go to prison and Yano can end up in a foster home. Or you can take the blame, for all of it. Gina and Yano can spend the rest of their days living lives of luxury, with me, working on the next *Space Corps* movie.

STANLEY: Have you lost your goddamn mind?

(Police sirens can be dimly heard, steadily increasing in volume.)

STANLEY: Holy shit, did you really call the cops?

BRUCE: Here's what we're going to say happened: you kidnapped me on your own. Just you. Nobody else. You kept Gina in the dark for years.

YANO: And me.

BRUCE: You, alone, killed Sherman Schneider. I sat in the boiler room listening to his screams and his begging right up until the moment you cut his throat. It was a nightmare.

STANLEY: I would never—

BRUCE: Your wife and son just recently found out, about everything. You told them you had silverfish. But they just learned: you had me locked down here all along? You killed Sherman down here? Who are you? You're a monster. They are terrified of you!

(The sirens stop.)

YANO: So scared.

STANLEY: I will deal with you later, you backstabbing little shit. *(To GINA)* Gina, stop this. This is ridiculous.

(Upstairs, the police start banging at the front door. An offstage POLICEMAN yells through the door:)

POLICEMAN: *(OS)* Open up! LAPD!

STANLEY: Gina!

BRUCE: Don't talk to her. She's made her choice.

STANLEY: I would like to hear that from my wife.

BRUCE: Ex-wife.

STANLEY: Fuck you!

BRUCE: This is happening, Stan. There's no stopping it. No matter what happens over the next two minutes, it's done. Either you go down, or we all do. You know which it has to be. You just don't fit in anymore, Stanley. The three of us believe in *Space Corps*. You just really, really like it.

POLICEMAN: *(OS)* Open up! Last warning!

(Upstairs, the police start banging away at the front door with a battering ram, slowly, loudly, methodically.)

BRUCE: That's the battering ram. It won't be long now.

STANLEY: Oh my God. What have you done? It's all over. All of our lives are over.

BRUCE: There is, of course, a third path open to us.

STANLEY: What is it?

(BRUCE points at the TS-620 still in STANLEY's hands.)

BRUCE: You could take that TS-620 rapid-repeat blaster rifle prop-accurate replica upstairs and point it while charging and screaming at the cops.

(Upstairs, the front door gets knocked in. Footsteps can be heard overhead as police enter the house.)

(SFX: police footsteps)

STANLEY: What?

BRUCE: It would greatly simplify things.

STANLEY: They'd shoot me.

YANO: You catch on fast, former dad.

STANLEY: *(To YANO)* You shut up!

BRUCE: Stanley. You invited me into your home, against my will. I used to be your prisoner, but now I have emasculated and replaced you. I am sleeping with your wife. I am surrogate father to your son. I am master of your domain. *Space Corps* is the destiny of this family, but this family no longer includes you. Again, Stan, this isn't personal, but you are expendable.

STANLEY: *(Quietly)* Oh, it's personal. *(He looks at* BRUCE*)* You're a murderer, Bruce. Not me. You. You killed Sherman Schneider! I had nothing to do with it. I'm a kidnapper. You're a killer. And now I'm gonna go up there and surrender myself and tell them the truth about what's been going on down here for all of these years.

BRUCE: For God's sake, why? Look around you. You have nothing left to live for.

STANLEY: Oh yes I do. My one goal in life, Bruce, is now to destroy you. We should have killed you when we kidnapped you. We should have dumped you in the river and gone on with our lives.

BRUCE: Maybe you should have. *(Pointing to the TS-620)* Be sure to point it right at them. And don't put it down, whatever they say.

STANLEY: Oh, yeah, I'll be sure to do just that.

GINA: Stanley!

STANLEY: Gina, I know things have gotten messed up, but we can fix this. We have to turn Bruce in. We have to—

GINA: Stanley.

STANLEY: Yes?

GINA: You're holding it wrong.

(It takes a beat for that to register with STANLEY, *and then he realizes what* GINA *means. He looks down, and finds he is indeed holding the TS-620 with one hand, as if it were a pistol.)*

STANLEY: I am.

GINA: You are. They'll never buy it if you hold it like that. All these years…

STANLEY: …and I still can't get it right.

GINA: You can't.

STANLEY: I loved you.

GINA: I know.

STANLEY: Wasn't that enough?

GINA: No.

(STANLEY *nods. He readjusts his grip on the prop weapon, and then he turns and exits into the house. There is silence for a moment, and then, offstage and from upstairs…*)

POLICEMAN: *(OS)* Sir! Drop the weapon! Drop it!

STANLEY: *(OS)* Yaaaaaahhhhhhhhh!

POLICEMAN: *(OS)* I SAID DROP IT!

(Gunshots ring out. Silence. A thud from above)

YANO: Yes!

BRUCE: Oh my god, I think it worked.

GINA: It's just the three of us now. As it should be.

BRUCE: You know, this might be something I should have brought up earlier, but… I don't know if I can say that I love you.

GINA: I don't know that I want you to.

BRUCE: Poor Stan. "Will the light shine his way—"

GINA: Don't. Don't waste it. We should get ready for the police. Back in the boiler room, quickly.

BRUCE: Are you all right?

GINA: This was the way it had to be.

BRUCE: But are you all right?

GINA: I am the way I have to be. For *Space Corps*.

BRUCE: Yes. For *Space Corps.*

(All three of them, BRUCE, GINA, and YANO join hands.)

BRUCE, GINA & YANO: For *Space Corps.*

(They bow their heads for a moment. GINA rests her head on BRUCE's shoulder. BRUCE kisses her on the top of the head. Finally, YANO looks up.)

YANO: Hey, dad?

BRUCE: Yes, son?

YANO: Can we bring Ding Dong Diggum back in *Chapter 7?*

BRUCE: We sure can, son.

(Horrified, GINA drops BRUCE's hand.)

GINA: Absolutely not!

(BRUCE and GINA stare each other down. Finally, BRUCE breaks the gaze and looks back at YANO.)

BRUCE: …We'll talk about it.

(Blackout)

END OF PLAY

www.ingramcontent.com/pod-product-compliance
Lightning Source LLC
Chambersburg PA
CBHW052202090426

42741CB00010B/2375